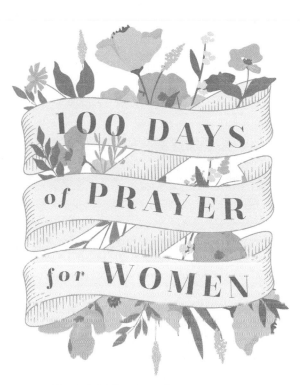

100 DAYS
of PRAYER
for WOMEN

Carolyn Larsen

Revell

a division of Baker Publishing Group
Grand Rapids, Michigan

Published by Revell
a division of Baker Publishing Group
PO Box 6287, Grand Rapids, MI 49516-6287
www.revellbooks.com

Printed in the United States of America

Library of Congress Cataloging-in-Publication Data
Names: Larsen, Carolyn, 1950– author.
Title: 100 days of prayer for women / Carolyn Larsen.
Other titles: One hundred days of prayer for women
Description: Grand Rapids, MI : Revell, a division of Baker Publishing Group, [2023]
Identifiers: LCCN 2022014282 | ISBN 9780800740825 (casebound) | ISBN 9781493439829 (ebook)
Subjects: LCSH: Christian women—Prayers and devotions.
Classification: LCC BV283.W6 L37 2023 | DDC 242/.843—dc23/eng/20220505
LC record available at https://lccn.loc.gov/2022014282

Unless otherwise indicated, Scripture quotations are from the *Holy Bible,* New Living Translation, copyright © 1996, 2004, 2007, 2013, 2015 by Tyndale House Foundation. Used by permission of Tyndale House Publishers, Inc., Carol Stream, Illinois 60188. All rights reserved.

Scripture quotations labeled CEV are from the Contemporary English Version © 1991, 1992, 1995 by American Bible Society. Used by permission.

Scripture quotations labeled ESV are from The Holy Bible, English Standard Version® (ESV®), copyright © 2001 by Crossway, a publishing ministry of Good News Publishers. Used by permission. All rights reserved. ESV Text Edition: 2016

Scripture quotations labeled The Message are from *THE MESSAGE*, copyright © 1993, 2002, 2018 by Eugene H. Peterson. Used by permission of NavPress. All rights reserved. Represented by Tyndale House Publishers, Inc.

Scripture quotations labeled NASB are from the (NASB®) New American Standard Bible®, Copyright © 1960, 1971, 1977, 1995, 2020 by The Lockman Foundation. Used by permission. All rights reserved. www.lockman.org

Scripture quotations labeled NCV are from the New Century Version®. Copyright © 2005 by Thomas Nelson. Used by permission. All rights reserved.

Scripture quotations labeled NIV are from THE HOLY BIBLE, NEW INTERNATIONAL VERSION®, NIV® Copyright © 1973, 1978, 1984, 2011 by Biblica, Inc.® Used by permission. All rights reserved worldwide.

23 24 25 26 27 28 29   7 6 5 4 3 2 1

Introduction

Dear reader,

If you have days when you need proof of God's amazing love for you, just think of the invitation he gives his children to talk with him. What an incredible privilege it is to be able to talk with the God of the Universe. It's not just that we *can* talk to him, but, even more amazing, he *asks* us to! He wants to know how we're feeling, what we're struggling with, what keeps us up at night. He wants to hear our praises. He wants to hear our thankfulness. He wants . . . us.

Scripture is filled with invitations to pray: "Do not be anxious about anything, but in everything by prayer and supplication with thanksgiving let your requests be made known to God" (Phil. 4:6 ESV). "Never stop praying" (1 Thess. 5:17). "Keep on asking, and you will receive what you ask for. Keep on seeking, and you will find. Keep on knocking, and the door will be opened to you" (Luke 11:9). "Call to me and I will answer you, and will tell you great and hidden things that you have not known" (Jer. 33:3 ESV). "I urge that supplications, prayers, intercessions, and thanksgivings be made for all people" (1 Tim. 2:1 ESV).

In fact, God says prayer is so important that he even makes provision for when we simply cannot find the words to pray: "The Holy Spirit helps us in our weakness. For example, we don't know what God wants us to pray for. But the Holy Spirit prays for us with groanings that cannot be expressed in words" (Rom. 8:26).

As believers, we can journey together in this life of faith. We are all in different places on the journey, but we have the responsibility and privilege of upholding one another in prayer. We have the privilege of interceding for those who are suffering or hurting. We have the joy of praising our God for all he does for us and how he blesses, guides, and loves us. Praise him in all things!

My hope is that these prayers—some of which are cries for his help, some of which are heartfelt praise—will spark your desires to reach out to God in praise, tears, hope, and love . . . whatever is on *your* heart.

Maybe you're a "read one prayer a day" kind of person, or perhaps you scan through several prayers looking for one that speaks to your heart on a given day. In the back of this book is an index of topics covered in these prayers. So, if you're lonely, afraid, anxious, confused, or filled with praise, check the index for a prayer that God may use to speak to your heart today.

Blessings,
Carolyn

1

A New Day

Dear Father,

Thank you for this new day after a good night of rest. I'm grateful for a clean slate where yesterday's attitudes are history and yesterday's sins are forgiven. A fresh start every day. Before my feet hit the floor each morning, I ask for your help to make this day better than yesterday. I need your strength to shut down my critical, judgmental, selfish attitudes. Oh God, muffle the sharp words that so easily fly out of my all-too-willing lips. Remind me that kindness matters . . . a lot, even when I don't think it's deserved. Remind me that life is not all about me.

Focus my thoughts and words on being the woman you want me to be, made me to be—a God-honoring servant who cares about others and reflects Jesus to everyone I meet. It's hard some days, God, but with all my heart . . . oh God, hear me . . . I long to make a difference for your kingdom. There's no way I can do that with my own uneven, flagrantly selfish behavior. So, in this new day, may your love, compassion, and kindness flow through me to every person who crosses my path.

Great is his faithfulness;
his mercies begin afresh each morning.

Lamentations 3:23

2

The Gift of Joy

My loving Father,

I'm so full of joy I may explode! That's amazing since I'm smack-dab in the middle of massive uncertainties and aware of heart-wrenching crises in our world. I've no idea what tomorrow will bring for any of us . . . yet I have real joy. It's certainly not because of anything I can take credit for. Oh sure, there are things that make me happy, but I know all too well that simple happiness runs away at the first sign of trouble. Joy though, joy bubbles up from the depths of my soul. It ignores worries, pain, failure, or crises.

Here's the thing, God, I know that joy comes only from your Spirit's presence in my heart. He prompts me with reminders that you are guiding my steps, my words, and even my thoughts. You're surrounding me and protecting me. You know everything about me. You love me in spite of my failures. Your unconditional love saves me, and you have a plan for my life that is grander than I could dream for myself. I own the privilege of praying to you, learning from your Word, and anticipating eternity with you. You give life meaning. Yes, what gives me joy is . . . you.

My lips will shout for joy
when I sing praise to you—
I whom you have delivered.
Psalm 71:23 NIV

3

Staying Connected

Lord,

I'm tired. No, that's not it. I'm weary. Bone weary. Every day I deal with the same things—get the kids up, dressed, fed, and out the door to school, make myself presentable for work, pick up the house, make dinner, clean the kitchen, monitor homework, and a thousand other things. Every day. Father, when is there time for me? When is there time to spend with you?

The "experts" say to get up earlier. But Lord, even if I get up ten minutes early, life inevitably interrupts. I dearly miss precious quiet time with you. I miss you.

I know life won't always be like this. In fact, someday I'll look back and think these years went by too quickly. But, for now, help me be creative in grabbing moments with you when I can. Help me think about you and talk with you while driving kids to soccer practice or waiting in line at the store. A thousand quick thoughts a day to keep me connected to you. And I will enjoy the quiet times I do get with you. Help me stick close to you through the weariness of these days even as I anticipate the future when I will miss the busyness of these days.

Come near to God, and God will come near to you

James 4:8 NCV

4

An Amazing Gift

Oh my God,

Thank you, thank you . . . just . . . thank you . . . for forgiveness . . . for second chances . . . for your love that is deeper and stronger than I can comprehend. Thank you for hope, for giving me strength when I have none left, for grace that meets me where I am and then grows me and moves me forward, for faith to believe that you have a wonderful, unique plan for my life. Thank you for seeing the deep desires of my heart more than the failures of my outward behavior. Thank you that even when I fall short of obeying you and disappoint myself in the process, you refuse to give up on me.

The truth is, you believe in me more than I believe in myself. That's an amazing gift! You've seen my past, forgiven and forgotten it, and now you are moving me toward a better future—a better me. My hope is in you. My heart is for you. My gratitude is more than I can put into words. I'm totally unworthy and yet totally blessed. Thank you. Thank you. Thank you.

Give thanks to the LORD, for he is good;
his love endures forever

1 Chronicles 16:34 NIV

5

Honest, Deep Faith

Oh dear God,

I know all the right words to say. I know when to act humble and when to act strong. I know how to sing praise. I know how to "act" Christian—and—I know when I'm just acting. I've seen the "fake it 'til you feel it" memes. And yes, I know I can't base faith on feelings. But, Lord, (big sigh) I'm tired of just acting. I want to stop just putting on a good outward show. Instead, I want to know you with a real, deep, strong, and trusting faith. I want to be honest with you and with myself even when that means owning up to my control issues and constant (why is it so constant?) struggle to believe and trust.

Faith is a journey, and honestly, that too often means two steps forward, then a tumble back. But that's okay because you understand that my heart yearns to know, love, and trust you. I know you'll help me brush off the dust of disappointment, grief, or failure and start moving forward again.

Thanks for not giving up on me. Thanks for loving me so much. And help me remember your constant love when I take one of those tumbles.

Search me, O God, and know my heart!
Try me and know my thoughts!

Psalm 139:23 ESV

6

Thankful for the Word

Father,

Your Word is such an incredible gift. I find deep comfort in its stories showing how you interacted with your people. Your compassion for them shines through clearly. I see how you cared about their pain and their problems. I love reading how you directed their lives, step-by-step, and even guided the words they spoke to pharaohs and Pharisees. It's also clear that you insisted they obey you. They were convicted of their sins by your Holy Spirit and then forgiven for those sins when they repented and punished when they didn't!

Each time I open my Bible, their stories come to life in new and life-relevant ways. Sometimes a verse I've read many times before seems to light up on the page because it's just what I needed for that day.

Father, I love your Word. I do. But sometimes I take it for granted and begin to drift away from reading it. I ask you to grow an active hunger for it in my heart. A hunger that draws me to it every day. A hunger that makes it so real and so necessary that your words are impressed on my heart and mind. Teach me through it. Guide me by it. Make your presence more alive and real to me through it.

Your word is a lamp for my feet,
a light on my path.

Psalm 119:105 NIV

7

Stubborn Hope

My dear, loving God,

What would I do without hope? This world is sometimes just too much. Too much anger. Too much division. Too much hatred. Too much trouble. Too much pain. Just too much. It's so easy to let my mind and heart get caught up in all that "too much," and then I become so weighed down that I lose all hope of things getting better. I confess to you that I too easily let my heart get sidetracked from trusting you. I get stuck on all the "too much" things and forget the hope of a better tomorrow.

My hope comes from you because all things come from you. My loving Father, the author and creator of hope, forgive my sidetracked thoughts. Forgive my hopelessness. Help me turn my heart to you. Help me be stubborn to keep my eyes firmly focused on you; stubborn to stay in your Word; stubborn to deny the lies the Evil One whispers; stubborn to trust you and be filled with peace because you promise hope.

You keep your promises, so I believe things *will* get better. I believe in hope because I trust you.

I pray that God, the source of hope, will fill you completely with joy and peace because you trust in him. Then you will overflow with confident hope through the power of the Holy Spirit.

Romans 15:13

8

A Praise-Filled Life

Father,

I praise you. I praise you for blue skies. I praise you for gray skies. I praise you for green grass and colorful flowers. I praise you for bare trees and dirty snow mounds. I praise you for oceans, lakes, and rivers. I praise you for mountains, deserts, and prairies. I praise you for husbands and children. I praise you for life itself. I praise you for beautiful music. I praise you for silence. I praise you for new life. I praise you for life ended. I praise you for sin forgiven. I praise you for obedience commanded. I praise you for joy-filled, happy days. I praise you for heart-wrenching days of sadness. I praise you for holiday tables mounded with delicious food. I praise you for humble one-dish meals. I praise you for laughter. I praise you for tears. I praise you for seeing my heart—the good of it and the bad of it. I praise you for all things because all things come from you. I praise you for your moment-by-moment presence. I praise you for your constant, steady, forgiving, grace-filled love that never lets me go. I praise you, Father, for all you are and all you so generously give!

Praise the LORD!

Give thanks to the LORD, for he is good!
His faithful love endures forever.

Psalm 106:1

9

Check-Mark Living

Oh dear Lord,

My life has become crazy busy. I'm literally living by check marks—checking things off my daily to-do list. Skating through chores, job, friends, but not really "being there" because as I'm completing one obligation (oh Lord, when did family and friends become an obligation?) I'm already moving toward the next thing on the list. This isn't really living, is it? I'm so busy that I'm missing who and what I should really be busy with.

Who? First of all you, Lord. I want time with you to talk, meditate, praise, and just tell you what's on my heart. I do love you.

My family. Oh God, I love them with all my heart. I want to show them that by spending good, quality time with them. Laughing. Talking. Loving.

Friends who enrich my life so much. I want to be compassionate to their struggles and celebrate their joys.

What? Whatever you direct me to do. Whatever you keep so obviously in front of me that I know it's what you want me to put my energy toward.

Help me get these priorities straight so I can do away with the check marks controlling my life. Thank you for your patience with me and guidance for me.

Seek the Kingdom of God above all else, and live righteously, and he will give you everything you need.

Matthew 6:33

10

Counting My Blessings

Dear Father,

Counting my blessings changes everything. That sounds like such an old-fashioned term, but I'm learning that actually doing it changes the trajectory of my day. Help me, Lord, to start my day with blessing number one—before I even get out of bed—to thank you for a new day. I will thank you for a night of rest and for waking me to this new day.

Looking for blessings throughout my day means there's little time to complain or wish away my day. I'm pretty good at noticing the big blessings you give me, such as your Word, forgiveness, grace, hope, eternity. But please don't let me forget the simple things that I so easily take for granted—my home, my job, coffee, food, warm slippers, flowers, sunrises, sunsets, laughter, music, friendship, and so much more. Even on the days when some of those things aren't working so well, I want to be grateful for them. All are gifts from you every single day. You made all things for me to enjoy.

Thank you for your blessings, and help me notice more and more of them every day. Big and small. I want my heart to overflow with gratitude.

Every good and perfect gift is from above, coming down from the Father of the heavenly lights, who does not change like shifting shadows.

James 1:17 NIV

11

Prayer for Remembrance

Oh Lord,

I long to sense your presence . . . to know you are paying attention to every moment, every situation I'm facing. I ache to remember that because I'm scared, and I need assurance that you are guiding my uncertain steps and my faltering speech. I know you've promised that, Lord . . . I do. It's just that sometimes I feel so far away from you and then . . . well, it's hard. I get confused and afraid. I need to know you're walking the pathway with me, even going ahead of me.

Help me trust. Help me grab on to the promises in your Word. Loving Father, fill my heart with the reality of your strength and power. Help me remember that nothing is happening in my life right now that surprises you. Remind my struggling heart that there's no reason to be frightened because I can trust that you are in control. Of course, I know you are, Lord, but I'm worn down to the point that my tired, aching heart needs a reminder of your comfort and encouragement.

Oh Father, I need your help to keep my mind and heart centered on you, depending on and trusting in you. Thank you for hearing my prayer.

Do not be anxious about anything, but in every situation, by prayer and petition, with thanksgiving, present your requests to God. And the peace of God, which transcends all understanding, will guard your hearts and your minds in Christ Jesus.

Philippians 4:6–7 NIV

12

Complete Trust

Dear Father,

I confess that I spend way too much of my prayer time telling you what to do. I know you care about the things I'm worried about and afraid of. You care about the things that keep me awake at night. But where my prayers collapse is that instead of just telling you about a problem or worry—you know, giving it to you and then walking away, trusting that you will handle it in the best possible way—I bring up the topic and then spend the next half hour telling you how to fix it. It's like I think I've come up with a better plan than you can. There's no trust in that behavior . . . only control issues and incredible arrogance. I'm so sorry.

Trusting you means believing that you can see over the mountain I'm trying to climb. You see the path ahead. You know what's on the other side. You have a plan that will help me and anyone else involved learn more about you and grow a deeper, stronger faith.

So I'll try to stop giving you a to-do list and instead just tell you what's on my heart and then leave it. You'll handle it in your way in your time. I trust you.

Trust GOD from the bottom of your heart;
don't try to figure out everything on
your own.

Proverbs 3:5 The Message

13

The Difference between Want and Need

Father,

You give me absolutely everything I need, though not everything I want. It for sure takes me a while to understand the difference. But for that brief moment when I do get it (because, let's just be honest, sometimes the understanding is fleeting), my heart is filled with peace and gratitude. But then the "wants" win out again and I start living like a duck in the water—looking calm on the surface, but underwater my big old feet are paddling for all I'm worth. I burn so much time and energy trying to get all my wants by myself instead of settling down into how you meet my actual needs.

I guess I could try to blame this on today's culture that relentlessly shouts how I have to be independent and self-sufficient and all that. But . . . it's really just sin. It's my sin. My failure to trust. My failure to be satisfied. My controlling spirit. I'm sorry, Father. Life would be so much easier if I could just let go and appreciate the way you meet my needs. Appreciating all you do will help me forget about my selfish wants and be grateful for all you give.

God will meet all your needs according to the riches of his glory in Christ Jesus.

Philippians 4:19 NIV

14

The Sweeter You Grow

Father,

I love Bill Gaither's old gospel song that says, "The longer I serve him, the sweeter he grows." I'm finding that to be very true. Thank you, Father, for picking me up when I fall flat on my face (time and time again). Thank you for brushing off the cobwebs and welcoming me home when it's been so very long since I've made time to be with you. Thank you for giving me your strength when I have none. Thank you for filling me with your joy when I can't find any on my own. Thank you for guiding me through life when everything around me seems dark and murky. Thank you for loving me even when I can't love myself—especially then. Thank you for forgiving me over and over again. Thank you for your grace and mercy. Thank you for seeing deep into my heart when my actions and words don't reflect its desires. Thank you for difficult times that teach me to lean on you. Thank you for cleaning up messes that my impetuousness causes. Thank you that it's really true that you grow sweeter and more precious to me with every single day.

How precious is your unfailing love,
    O God!
All humanity finds shelter
    in the shadow of your wings.

Psalm 36:7

15

Identity in God

Oh God,

Help me remember that I am not who others say I am. I do not need to live up (or down) to their expectations of me. I do not need to fit tidily into the little boxes that others construct for me because I do not answer to them. I answer only to you. I am who you say I am—I am made in your image and uniquely gifted by you. I am challenged to do the specific work you put before me. My heart and conscience are guided by your Spirit. The situations, crises, and relationships that break my heart are because you move me to that deep, caring level of heartbreak.

Oh Father, keep moving me forward to become the woman you've created me to be—even if that doesn't neatly fit into what others expect of me or for me. Keep opening my heart to what's true and real, even if that truth sometimes makes me uncomfortable. And yes, even if that truth makes others uncomfortable. I long for my faith walk to be wild, exciting, risk-taking, and uniquely mine! Let's go, Father, let's go!

We neither make nor save ourselves. God does both the making and saving. He creates each of us by Christ Jesus to join him in the work he does, the good work he has gotten ready for us to do, work we had better be doing.

Ephesians 2:7–10 The Message

16

God's Precious Presence

Father,

Big sigh. I've spent the last few days wallowing in self-pity and feeling bad that I am so alone. My friends haven't picked up on my loneliness. I mean, they aren't calling or stopping by, are they? How many big deep sighs do I have to sigh? I want to shout, "Hey you all—I'M LONELY! I NEED YOU." Oh right . . . there's no one around to hear my sighs or shouts.

Yes, that's how my pity party has gone. But then I remembered that I'm actually not alone because you are here. You hear my every sigh, every word I utter, every thought I think. I ask you to forgive me, God. Forgive the pity party that makes me forget you're always here. I'm not alone—ever. How precious that is! Help me to find fulfillment, comfort, companionship in you. And when others are around me, I will appreciate their presence while remembering that they are a gift from you. I'll be grateful for them and the joy of having people with me. But Father, help me always find my company, companionship, fulfillment, and comfort in you. All other— human—company is just icing on the cake!

I am convinced that neither death, nor life, nor angels, nor principalities, nor things present, nor things to come, nor powers, nor height, nor depth, nor any other created thing will be able to separate us from the love of God that is in Christ Jesus our Lord.

Romans 8:38–39 NASB

17

True Peace

Oh God,

If I'm honest (and I guess I will be), I may look to others like I'm serene and peaceful and fully trusting you, but in reality that's just on the surface. Why can't I actually BE serene and peaceful? Family issues keep me in a turmoil. Friend problems are upsetting. My job is tenuous at best.

These things are all upsetting, but I have to acknowledge that the true reason I have no peace is because I don't fully trust you to handle my problems. You know how I think—if "this" happens, then everything will be great.

If "that person" settles down, then life will be peaceful. I don't know why I keep doing this. I know it doesn't help. In my heart I know that when I just trust you with ALL things, then you handle everything and I can be filled with peace. Yes, my heart knows that, but my mind takes off on a tangent with all the "what ifs" because I'm so good at worry.

I'm tired of the constant, frantic worry. Help me, God, to bring everything to you and just leave my worries and problems there. I long for the peace that comes only from trusting you.

> You, LORD, give true peace
>   to those who depend on you,
>   because they trust you.
>   Isaiah 26:3 NCV

18

Time for Confession

Dear Father,

Confession isn't easy for me. I suppose it isn't easy for anyone. I mean, I think I'm a pretty good person, so there isn't that much to confess. On the other hand, I know I could sit before you confessing all day and still not get everything out in the open.

With a little fear (and a lot of trembling) I ask you to look deep into my heart. I know what you'll find there: disobedience, selfishness, rebellion, control issues, and all kinds of other things, even (embarrassingly) apathy. These are things I've gotten so used to that I justify them away.

Oh God, open my eyes. Help me face what I need to face and what I need to confess. Let me see the things in my thoughts, my words, my actions, and my attitudes that grieve you. I can't change what I haven't faced. Father, I really want you to show me that it's not just "other" people who sin. Sin is alive and well in my life too, and it's time for me to stop excusing my actions, words, and thoughts. That's the only way I'm going to become more like Jesus, and becoming more like him is exactly what I want.

If we say that we have not sinned, we are fooling ourselves, and the truth isn't in our hearts. But if we confess our sins to God, he can always be trusted to forgive us and take our sins away.

1 John 1:8–9 CEV

19

Stop Me from Being Impetuous

Dear Father,

There are so many blogs, podcasts, and books with messages calling women to "be real." "Be your true self." "Look out for number one." They warn me against letting myself be pressed into someone else's idea of worth, success, Christianity, wifehood, motherhood, or friendship. Be willing, they say, to let go of anyone who tries to hold me back.

I don't want to be tethered to someone else's idea of how to live. Your plan for me is the one that matters. I have no doubt that there are some toxic relationships I need to deal with. But what I want to be careful of, and what I ask your discernment and wisdom for, is that you keep me from shedding people I shouldn't be shedding. Give me the wisdom to realize that a minute's unhappiness or frustration is not a good enough reason to push someone out of my life. Lord, give me discernment. Give me the patience to see the importance of someone in my life over the long term, even if there are short-term frustrations. Give me wisdom to know who to walk away from, who to cling to, and who to pray for. Please keep me from impetuous, knee-jerk reactions to someone else's message.

You can trust a friend
who corrects you,
but kisses from an enemy
are nothing but lies.
Proverbs 27:6 CEV

20

I Choose God

Almighty God,

I choose you. The voices of the world bombard me with their definitions of worth. They tempt me to make other things more important than you. But no, I choose you. The world shouts that my worth is found in a successful career of climbing a corporate ladder, making lots of money, wielding power through seemingly important decisions. But no, I choose you. The world maintains that I find identity in marriage, being a devoted wife, supporting my husband's needs, having children to whom I devote all my energy by volunteering at school, driving to sports practices or music rehearsals, losing myself in them. But no, I choose you.

Oh God, of course there's nothing wrong with any of those things. I know that. They are good. They are rewarding. They are important. I'm pleased that some of those things are part of my life. But God, I know that nothing, absolutely nothing can be more important than you. What is important is what you have chosen for my life. All other things are seen through the filter of my devotion to you. What defines my value and worth is simply that I am your daughter. You are my God. I choose you before all other things. I am yours.

Even before he made the world, God loved us and chose us in Christ to be holy and without fault in his eyes.

Ephesians 1:4

21

Help Me Forgive

Oh God,

I'm hurt, angry, confused, and even scared. I trusted my friend, but my trust was betrayed. I thought we respected each other. I thought the trust was mutual. It wasn't, and now I feel alone and like I'm drifting. I don't know what to do with these feelings. I just want to . . . I don't know . . . make my friend hurt as much as I hurt. I know that's not right, but I need you to help me, God . . . please.

Keep me from speaking angry, hurtful words. Keep reminding me that spouting my pain to all the world won't make it go away, but it will damage any possible restoration of this relationship. Attempting to destroy my friend's reputation won't stop the hurt. Asking others to take my side will not really speak well of me. Stop me from lashing out in anger and saying things that can't be taken back, forgotten, or forgiven. Two wrongs do not make a right. Other people will be hurt by my angry words—not just this friend and not just me.

God, I ask you for the strength to forgive, even if there's no repentance. Forgive through me when I don't have the strength to do it myself. I ask you to help me let go of the hurt. I ask you to calm my anger. It serves no good and hurts only me. I hurt, God. I hurt so much. Please help me get through this. I pray for my friend too. God, work in both of our hearts. Restore our relationship.

---

*The LORD is close to the brokenhearted
and saves those who are crushed in
spirit.*

Psalm 34:18 NIV

22

Protection for Those in Danger

Almighty, powerful, loving God,
Today I pray for your grace and strength to fill the hearts of believers around this world who are in grave danger simply because they follow you. God, protect them from their enemies, meet their daily needs, fill them with your peace and a sense of your presence, bless them with grace to help them face challenges and losses. Be especially close to children who lose parents and family members. Father, may an awareness of your love and presence draw them to you

rather than their losses driving them away from you. Grant your mercy to protect your people. But if their lives are to be taken because of their faith, may your grace give them peace and courage as they come to you. Grant them a joyful anticipation of the reward of being with you and bravery as they leave this earth.

God, may the persecutors be softened to stop the evil they are doing. If not, I pray they will answer to you for what they have done. I know they will.

Father, may we never take for granted our freedom to worship. I confess that all too often, I do. Help me remember that there are some who do not have that freedom. Oh God, may I never stop praying for their courage, their protection, and their witness for you.

Fear not, for I am with you;
   be not dismayed, for I am your God;
I will strengthen you, I will help you,
   I will uphold you with my righteous
      right hand.

                              Isaiah 41:10 ESV

23

Thankful for God's Goodness

Oh God,

On the days when the clouds hang so low that they make it hard to breathe . . . on the days when I feel lost and alone . . . on the days when I question if you're even paying attention . . . on those dark days, oh God, help me remember that you are always good. You are good even when what's happening doesn't seem to be good. You are present, even when I can't sense your presence. You are leading, even when I can't see where I'm going. Your promises are true, even when I don't understand what's happening. You are unchanging, even in a world that's changing minute by minute. Your Word is pure. Your love is unconditional, constant, and grace-filled, even when I don't feel lovable. Your plan is eternal, for all people, even me. Your forgiveness is real, even though I don't deserve it. Your grace is undeniable, even though I can't understand it.

Thank you for having a plan for my life. Thank you for loving me so much that you're willing to let me hurt because that's how I learn to become dependent on you and trust you more fully. Thank you for never turning away from me. Thank you for your goodness. Thank you for your love.

Give thanks for everything to God the Father in the name of our Lord Jesus Christ.

Ephesians 5:20

24

Letting Go of Anger

Dear Father,

Why is it so hard to forgive? I try, and I think I've done it, but then I slide back to anger and hurt. So I guess I never really forgave at all. I recognize that I'm punishing myself more than the one who hurt me. This struggle has made me realize how self-focused I am—how I manage to bring any situation around to me and my feelings or agenda instead of trying to understand where the other person is coming from.

Father, I need your help. Remind me that life isn't all about me and my feelings. Help me understand others' motives and care about their feelings. Help me want to forgive. After all, you forgive me over and over, even though I don't deserve it. Father, I can't do this on my own. I'm too weak, too self-centered.

What a relief to know that I have the greatest forgiver ever to guide and strengthen me. Thank you that you forgive me for being unforgiving. Thank you for seeing that my heart wants to forgive but needs your help to make it reality. Thank you that your forgiveness can flow through me if I allow it.

Be kind and compassionate to one another, forgiving each other, just as in Christ God forgave you.

Ephesians 4:32 NIV

25

Help in the Busyness of Life

Dear God,

I feel like I'm the frosting in a layer cake. I'm sandwiched between a layer of being a good daughter to aging parents, and a layer of being a good wife to the guy I love but just don't seem to have time for, and a layer of being a good mother to busy kids with homework, sports, and music practices. I don't even know what to say about maintaining friendships, taking care of a house, my own job, and . . . okay, that's enough.

Oh Father, I feel fragmented, and I wonder if I'm doing a good job with any of this. I'm tired. I'm worried. I'm pressed. I know, I know, this is a stage of life and someday I'll look back on these as the good old days (I hope). In the meantime, God, I'm afraid that the weight of those layers is literally squeezing out the sweetness of my relationship with you, my relationships with others, and even my opinion of myself.

Lord, help me prioritize what's important each day. Show me what I need to let go of. Help me cut myself some slack and just do the best I can and enjoy this stage of life. Father, I don't want to miss the sweetness of moments, the joy of being present with the people I love, and the pleasure of things I enjoy.

Come to me, all you who are weary and burdened, and I will give you rest.

Matthew 11:28 NIV

26

Open My Eyes, Lord

Oh God,

The last few years have brought so many issues, not the least of which is a deadly virus that has killed many and brought fear, financial loss, and isolation. Oh God, so many people are hurting, scared, or just plain lonely, longing for face-to-face human contact and the comfort of an actual hug.

Lord, I ask you to give me a compassionate heart to notice those who are lonely, hurting, or scared. But Lord, I want to do more than just notice—I want to actually do something. I ask you to give me sensitivity in knowing what to do and how to do it, whether you direct me to help through acts of friendship, like a phone call, picking up groceries for a neighbor, sending cards, or anything else that's needed, or maybe all I can do (the best thing to do) is pray for others. Whatever you direct, remind me to treat all with kindness and to respect their dignity.

Lord, I don't want to be like the Pharisees, who made everything about themselves. Open my eyes to those who need friendship or help of any kind. Direct my words and my actions so that they see you through all I do and say. You. Not me.

Two are better than one,
    because they have a good return for
        their labor:
If either of them falls down,
    one can help the other up.
But pity anyone who falls
    and has no one to help them up.

Ecclesiastes 4:9–10 NIV

27

Longing to Know You, Father

Oh God,

Forgive me, but sometimes I wonder if plain, old, nothing-special me could really be important to you. And because I have these thoughts, I think I must be on your B-team. I mean, I know you love me. But I see others serving you with confidence and passion. They seem to have a clear view of what you want from them. Some seem to get direct messages from you, as though you speak aloud to them. Their relationship with you is so tight and intimate. Oh God, I want that! But, I don't have it . . . yet.

I want to trust you with everything in my life. I want to be completely submitted to you, which will make that trust real and foundational. I want a crazy faith that makes me courageous and brave.

Show me how, Lord. Show me how to obey, love, learn, grow, and trust. Stop me from getting stuck in the comparison cycle. Instead, help me obey what I know and trust that my obedience is good enough for today and that it will grow for tomorrow. Oh Lord, I long to know you more deeply and serve you more fully. I long to be a part of your work in this world

---

*I knew you before I formed you in your
      mother's womb.
   Before you were born I set you apart
   and appointed you as my prophet to
      the nations.*

Jeremiah 1:5

28

I Need You, Lord

Father,

When my head hits the pillow at night, the worry/ stress/fear monster wakes up. One stressful scenario after another of "what if," "why not," or "why did I?" races through my thoughts. Worry, stress, and fear leave no chance for sleep or peace. I wish I could just crawl into your lap, Jesus, and just . . . be. I want to just rest in your presence, sensing, knowing your comfort and love.

I believe that your presence in my heart means peace, Lord. The moments when I am able to slow my racing mind and stop fretting and worrying . . . when I can just "be" and focus on your presence, well, that's when I actually have peace. Father, help me concentrate on your words of promise about peace, trust, and protection. Help me remember that your presence is constant and is more powerful than any of the things I'm stressing about. In reality, most of those things will never actually happen anyway. Even if they do, you can handle them. You have promised to do that for me if I will just trust you.

You, Lord. I only need you. You will give me peace.

I have told you all this so that you may have peace in me. Here on earth you will have many trials and sorrows. But take heart, because I have overcome the world.

John 16:33

29

Thankful for God's Love

My loving Father,

You are so good to me. Always so good. You are patient. You are loving. You are faithful. You are consistent. You are forgiving. You are grace-filled. Each time I trust you and leave my problems and worries with you instead of trying to plow through them on my own, you take care of them. Maybe you don't do things in the way I imagined, but you always handle things in the way that's best for me in the long run. Just like you promised! Your plan is always better than mine. Always. Thank you for always choosing the better plan.

Thank you for providing loving correction when I wander and for doing what you must to keep me on the right track. Thank you for never giving up on me. Sometimes the lessons hurt, but I know you are lovingly growing me into the person you know I can be. Sometimes the hurt is from discipline. Sometimes it is for a lesson. But it is always for my good. Eventually I see the love in all you do.

I praise you for how well you love me, Lord. You are so good.

My child, don't reject the LORD's discipline,
and don't be upset when he corrects
you.
For the LORD corrects those he loves,
just as a father corrects a child in
whom he delights.

Proverbs 3:11–12

30

Teach Me, Lord

Oh Lord,

Forgive me for thinking I have "arrived," for believing I have a handle on obeying you, for assuming I have everything figured out. How arrogant. Oh God, my heart is willing and eager to obey you and show your love through my thoughts, my words, and my life, but okay, I know that I haven't arrived. I know I'm slowly climbing up a learning curve.

When I met Jesus, I enthusiastically hit the ground running, forgetting that I was a child, a baby even, with much to learn. Teach me how to submit to you. Show me how to let go of control. Remind me to stop and think before blurting out unkind words. Help me wait on your guidance and direction. Slow me down so I take time to listen to your Spirit speaking through my thoughts and feelings. Remind me that I'm still learning, will always be learning. Help me believe that today I am enough in how I'm obeying you. Remind me that tomorrow I will be even "more enough" because my faith walk is a journey.

I am grateful that you're teaching me through your unending, amazing, constant love.

Train me, GOD, to walk straight;
then I'll follow your true path.
Put me together, one heart and mind;
then, undivided, I'll worship in joyful
fear.
From the bottom of my heart I thank
you, dear Lord;
I've never kept secret what you're up to.
You've always been great toward me—
what love!

Psalm 86:11–13 The Message

31

Have Your Way, Lord

Oh God,

I'm confused, sad, scared, and yes, embarrassed. Our social media–infested world is confusing and scary. There's so much criticism, judgment, and downright hatred tossed around. Some of it even comes from those who think they know how you feel and what you want to happen. They are so sure that you want a particular political party to have power and that if that doesn't happen, our country and even our world will be destroyed. The people saying these things are good people, and those with opposite opinions are good people too. Still, families and friendships are being torn apart over these things. Standing for biblical principles is good and right, but God, shouldn't we do so with respect for others?

God, you are all-powerful. Nothing happening in our world—politically, socially, medically—none of it surprises you. You know where we're headed, even as we battle the god of this world. You know the end result. You can use any situation or any person to bring people's hearts to you, and that's what is most important. Father, help me keep my heart focused simply on knowing you more deeply, obeying you, loving others, being kind and compassionate. And God, have your way in this world.

---

*We humans keep brainstorming options
and plans,
but God's purpose prevails.*

Proverbs 19:21 The Message

32

Loving Myself

Dear heavenly Father,

One thing I think I'm pretty good at is loving other people. You made it very clear in your Word that I should love others, so I know that's important to you. I care when someone is struggling or hurting. I take time to listen to them. I'm willing to go out of my way to help others, giving my time, energy, and even money.

But something I've come to realize is that one thing I'm *not* good at is loving myself. I'm so critical of me. I often feel I'm not smart enough, good enough, obedient enough, faithful enough. My opinion of myself paralyzes me.

I don't give myself the benefit of the doubt as I do for others. I don't give myself care the way I do for others.

God, the reality is that when I don't love myself, I am criticizing your creation. You made me the way you want me to be, and while I should study and learn and pray in order to become the best version of myself, I should also accept and appreciate the talents, gifts, interests, and abilities you uniquely gave me. Help me learn to love and appreciate myself and to believe you do love me exactly as I am.

I praise you because I am fearfully and
wonderfully made;
your works are wonderful,
I know that full well.

Psalm 139:14 NIV

33

Thankful for My Friends

My loving Father,

I am so very thankful for friends. You knew how much I would need them, and you gave me exactly the right ones. Some are social friends, who I enjoy because we share interests, laughter, and fun through activities, book clubs, or gym workouts. Some are more acquaintances, whose friendly hello and warm smile can be uplifting on a dark day. Some are inner-circle friends, who walk with me through the hard times, crying with me, praying with me, and holding me up when I feel I can't stand. They also celebrate with me when things are good and encourage me to keep going when I feel stuck or to rest when I'm tired.

The deepest friends share my love for you. We encourage each other in our faith journeys. I can trust my deepest secrets with the friends who know me well. These friends don't judge my words or actions, yet they kindly hold me accountable to being a true Jesus follower and a good friend. They challenge me to keep growing and learning. They help me up when I stumble.

Friends, God, are gifts from you, and each one enhances different aspects of my life. Thank you for every single one of them.

Friends love through all kinds of weather,
and families stick together in all kinds
of trouble.

Proverbs 17:17 *The Message*

34

Keep Me Close to You

My precious Father,

Please hold me close. Oh God, I need you. I need your strength. I need your protection. Father, take my face in your hands and turn my eyes toward you. Hold me, Father, gently but firmly. Keep my eyes and heart from wandering to things Satan dangles in front of me—things that look appealing but that pull my trust and devotion away from you.

Satan is just evil. He tries to tempt me with things that look good and even innocent . . .

things like the approval and praise of others, or things I could have if only I relax my focus of obeying you. I admit it's sometimes tempting. I even admit that sometimes I give in. The things he throws at me are distracting. It can be quite confusing. But Lord, I long to serve you and not be tricked by Satan's distractions.

In the words of the old hymn, help me to intentionally, moment by moment, turn my eyes upon Jesus and "look full in his wonderful face." That's the only path to true peace and joy. Oh Father, help me to resist the sneaky work of the Evil One. Help me to stay focused, stay true, stay committed to you.

Stay alert! Watch out for your great enemy, the devil. He prowls around like a roaring lion, looking for someone to devour.

1 Peter 5:8

35

Helping Others

Oh God,

I struggle with things like why children starve to death, die from lack of clean water, or are homeless. Of course, there are adults who experience all these things too, but God . . . children? Those seem like easy things you could fix. I mean, you gave manna to your people and you helped Moses get water from a rock. Why do some people have so very little when others (me) have more than they need? It's hard to see how those hungry, thirsty, homeless people can know your love through their struggles. Why don't you improve their situations and fix their problems? Then they might put their faith in you.

Wait a minute. What? I should help? You've blessed me so that I may bless others? Okay, I get that your people have a responsibility to help others. To whom much is given, much is required.

Lead me to ministries that help the hungry, thirsty, or homeless. Give me courage to care for the hurting and grieving. Help me be a friend to the lonely. Show me how to help the sick. Father, don't let me be apathetic about this. You said I should love others, and this is one way I can put action to those words.

We love because God loved us first.

1 John 4:19 CEV

36

Thankful for Salvation

Oh God,

I am always quick to pour out my requests to you, and I always have many. Sometimes I remember to thank you for the many blessings you've given me—my home, family, friends, career, food, and water. But Father, I so often forget to thank you for the most precious blessing of all. I don't deserve any of your goodness, very least of all this one most important gift—salvation. I can't even comprehend how magnificent this gift is. I have no real concept of what the future would hold without it.

Your amazing love for me is shown by the sacrificial gift of your own Son. I'm thankful that because of Jesus I have the amazing promise of eternal life with you! And my sins, oh God, my sins—I fight so hard to stop them, but I fail over and over again. I am amazed that you forgive my sins daily because of your great love. Jesus paid the price for those sins, so you see my stumbling heart as clean and pure. Thank you. All the rest of life—every relationship, every experience, every hope, and every dream—is made alive by the salvation you have given me. My eternal future is secure with you because of your gift of salvation.

For God so loved the world that he gave his one and only Son, that whoever believes in him shall not perish but have eternal life.

John 3:16 NIV

37

The Bible
Is a Blessing

Dear heavenly Father,

Sometimes when I'm trying to learn something new I'm reminded of how grateful I am for the Bible. Learning how to live in a way that honors you and shows others what it means to be your daughter in this chaotic world is made so much easier because of the guidance and instruction of your Word. What a gift it is.

I take seriously the opportunity to memorize verses so that I can recall them (or the Holy Spirit can remind me of them). They give me the strength and courage to live in a "set apart" way. Your Word gives me strength and courage. It encourages me to be kind and loving, filled with grace toward others. Let's face it, that's not always my first line of behavior until your words remind me.

Your words promise me your moment-by-moment presence, your strength, your grace, your forgiveness. Your Word tells me all I need to know about you. It shows me how you interacted with your people. It shows me Jesus's love and compassion as well as his strength and truth. It also reminds me to be serious about my walk with you. I'm thankful for your Word and that your Spirit often brings your words to mind at exactly the right time to help me, encourage me, guide me, and save me from bad behavior or unkind treatment of others.

I have hidden your word in my heart,
that I might not sin against you.

Psalm 119:11

38

Nothing Is Impossible

Sovereign God,

I trust that nothing, absolutely nothing is impossible for you. Nothing in this universe can stand against your power. No person, no nation, no fake god can defeat you. You created all that's here. You keep the sun, moon, and stars in place. You command the wind. You care for the giant whale and the tiny hummingbird. No problem is too big. No situation is too complicated. No crisis is hopeless. Nothing surprises you. You see the end from the beginning in all things, even (especially) in my life—you know all that's ahead. You know my private motives in the depths of my heart, and you love me anyway. You know my thoughts before I think them and forgive me when they aren't loving and kind.

It gives me deep peace to know that nothing is impossible for you and with you. I can bring any problem, situation, relationship, fear, or worry to you, knowing that you can handle it . . . and will handle it according to your will, which is framed in boundless love.

Thank you, my God, for who you are and how you love. Thank you that absolutely nothing is impossible for you.

Jesus looked at them intently and said, "Humanly speaking, it is impossible. But with God everything is possible."

Matthew 19:26

39

Protect My Children, Lord

Dear Lord,

I love my children. Oh sure, they make me crazy sometimes, but I can't imagine life without them. They exhaust me and they energize me. They are so constant, yet I miss them when I'm away from them. They are a blessing and a responsibility.

Father, I really want to be a good mom. Help me be courageous enough to let them try new things and strong enough to let them learn from failing. That's not easy. I wonder if it's hard for you to let your children fail even though we learn from our failures. Help me be brave enough to encourage my children to try again and wise enough to help them know when that "thing" isn't for them.

My biggest prayer, Father, is that my children come to know you early so they have a lifetime of learning about you, and a lifetime of learning who they are in you, and a lifetime of serving you. I want them to know that you love them.

Father, protect them from the Evil One. But when they do encounter Satan, fill them with your wisdom, strength, and courage to push him away

Lord, grow them. Guide them. Strengthen them. Protect them. I know you love them even more than I do. I'm glad about that because that means they are living surrounded in love.

I have loved you, my people, with an everlasting love.
With unfailing love I have drawn you to myself.

Jeremiah 31:3

40

Help Me Live in the Now

Oh God,

I'm wishing my life away. Some days my thoughts whisper, "When this stage of life is over then I'll . . ." or "Next year or in five years I'll do something important." Those thoughts keep me from living in the now, from being the woman you want me to be now, serving and loving those around me now.

Oh God, life is right now. There is purpose in today. I want to make the most of the life you've given me, Lord. I want to serve you and be a part of your incredible plan for this world today. If I'm always wishing to be in the next place or next stage, then I'm not being useful right now. Open my eyes, Father, to my world right now—to the people around me each moment—to notice where a kind word, a gentle smile, or a bit of encouragement might help someone. Open my heart to the needs that I can help meet for the lonely, the grieving, the needy. Show me where you want me to be and keep my attention and energy in the here and now. I know you've got something for me to do today and that however big or however small, it matters.

A body is made up of many parts, and each of them has its own use. That's how it is with us. There are many of us, but we each are part of the body of Christ, as well as part of one another.

Romans 12:4–5 CEV

41

Bless My Family and Friends

My loving Father,

I pray for my family and friends often, but lately I've realized that I usually pray for them to behave the way I want them to behave. I want them to do the things I want them to do, to value the things I value. I put the responsibility of our relationship health on them. I say I want them to meet me halfway, but actually I want them to share my viewpoints and do what I want. I'm praying selfish and self-centered prayers.

So today, Father, I pray for my family and friends to know your guidance in their lives. I pray for them to be strong in staying close to you. I pray for satisfaction and joy in their lives. I pray for them to be aware of your love and guidance. I pray for them to obey you, even if that means they do something or behave in a way that isn't what I want. Thank you for each of my family and friends. Thank you for their care for me. Thank you for laughter and quiet talks and even respectful disagreements. Thank you that they each care about living for you and serving you. Thank you that together we are a team. Help me to start acting like we are.

All of you, be like-minded, be sympathetic, love one another, be compassionate and humble.

1 Peter 3:8 NIV

42

Keeping My Thought Life in Check

Father,

I confess that I let my thoughts wander away from you once in a while, well, more than once in a while. That's never a good thing. My thoughts fixate on the "what ifs" of life or on perceived slights from others. Oh God, I confess that I can build a whole argument against a friend or loved one and they have absolutely no idea there is even a problem. It doesn't take long before I'm actually verbally attacking them and damaging our relationship in the process. The scary thing is that it all starts with just a thought. A thought that I don't push away. A thought that I let myself dwell on. Negative thoughts too easily lead to negative behavior.

Father, I need to keep my thoughts under control. I need to guard my mind. When a negative thought slips into my mind, help me examine it to see if what it's saying is true. If it is, then guide me in dealing with it in a mature, kind way. If it isn't, with your Spirit's help I have to cast it out. I have to. Help me to be kind and fair to others by guarding the thoughts I allow to take up residence in my mind and heart.

Dear brothers and sisters, one final thing. Fix your thoughts on what is true, and honorable, and right, and pure, and lovely, and admirable. Think about things that are excellent and worthy of praise.

Philippians 4:8

43

Thankful for Freedom

Father,

I'm going to be completely honest here . . . sometimes I'm not very grateful for what you do for me. There, I said it. Sometimes I ignore or even deny my selfishness, pride, anger . . . my sins. When I do, I am denying the magnitude of what you sacrificed to forgive my sin. I'm not admitting what it cost you. I'm so sorry. So very sorry that I let me get in the way of you.

Lord, I acknowledge right now your incredible grace, forgiveness, kindness, and sacrifice.

Through the agony of Jesus's life, torture, death, and resurrection I have been freed from the slavery of my sin. I've been given the hopeful promise of eternity with you. Unbelievable! Help me, Lord, to realize what that means—freedom from being chained to sin and death. A chain that I cannot break. I don't have the strength or power in any measure to gain my own freedom. I do not even have a partial conception of what that slavery meant. I don't have a real understanding of what an eternity separated from you would look like. I'm thankful that I don't have to know.

Thank you for Jesus. Thank you for forgiveness and grace and a multitude of second chances. Thank you for eternity in the freedom of your presence

---

He is so rich in kindness and grace that he purchased our freedom with the blood of his Son and forgave our sins.

Ephesians 1:7

44

Hungering for Jesus

Lord,

I sit here before you with a consuming hunger, but I don't really know what it is I hunger for. You know what it is though, because you can see more deeply into my heart than I can. Father, I pray for your Spirit to feed me, to show me what it is I hunger for. Father, meet me where I am, see the questions, doubts, fears, and needs in my heart.

Thank you for not giving up on me. Thank you for seeing sins hidden beneath the surface and for cleansing those sins. Sins that I don't even see, Father. Look deep into my heart and reveal more of what needs to be washed away. Show me where I fail. Show me where I fall. I know that I sometimes don't even realize my failures to obey . . . to follow . . . to love. I am often blinded to my own sin. Lord, open my eyes. Clean me. Feed me with the nutrition and power of your Word. Bury it in my heart so I will never forget and so its truth will grab me daily.

I love you, Lord. I hunger to know you more deeply, follow you more closely, and become more like you with each passing day.

Create in me a clean heart, O God,
and renew a right spirit within me.
Psalm 51:10 ESV

45

I Matter to Jesus

Lord,

As a woman, I've experienced the ongoing struggle to be valued . . . to be seen and heard in my work, friendships, and sometimes even in my closest relationships. While it's true that we've made a lot of progress in society, it's not fully right yet. In too many places, women still bounce against a glass ceiling. Women still battle for equal pay with men. Women still must work harder than ever to be heard, seen, and valued for our intelligence, creativity, and what we can contribute. We struggle for our voices to be heard.

Lord, I just want to thank you that Jesus SAW the women around him. So often we read that it was through women that his work was done, his message proclaimed and shared. It was women he trusted to first tell of his resurrection. It was often the women who were shamed and about to be punished in society whom he forgave. It was sometimes women who received his miracles and spoken forgiveness. He valued women. He loved them and gave them justice and grace. Lord, I hang on to the truth that as a believer and a woman, I matter to Jesus, and that's all that matters.

Look at the birds, free and unfettered, not tied down to a job description, careless in the care of God. And you count far more to him than birds.

Matthew 6:26 *The Message*

46

My God, My King

My Father God,

Today I honor you as my King. You are the servant King who sacrificially gave all for us, your children. You serve us by caring for us, providing for us, giving all to us.

I praise you as King of the Universe, whose power is beyond compare. Oh God, no ruler, no power, no nation, no leader can stand before you. Satan has no power against you. You, my God, are over all. One day every knee will bow before you and every tongue will acknowledge your power, strength, and love.

I submit to you as my Sovereign King. Nothing is outside your will. I may be stubborn and controlling of my own life, but, Father, either you allow me to have my own way so that I learn or you overcome my stubbornness to do what's best for me.

The earth itself submits to you. If your children didn't proclaim your name, the rocks themselves would do so. You are over all!

You are my loving King because even with all your power and strength (or because of it) I feel your love for me in every fiber of my being. I know your love in my darkest hour and in my happiest. You are King of my life.

To the King of the ages, immortal, invisible, the only God, be honor and glory forever and ever. Amen.

1 Timothy 1:17 ESV

47

Painful Growth

My loving Father,

You love me. I believe that. Your Word tells me over and over that you do. You want what's best for me. I believe that too. I know you are growing my faith and trust in you, and I want that. But I understand that kind of honest, deep growth usually happens when I'm going through difficult things. It comes through experiences when I must depend on you because you're the only person or thing that will get me through those hard times. Transformation, growth, learning, faith . . . well that doesn't really happen when life is smooth and easy, does it?

Father, I want the transformation. So I willingly submit to experiencing the difficulties and struggles in order for the growth to happen. Help me fight through the urge to run away or to try to change things on my own. Help me be still. Help me listen. Help me trust. Help me embrace the struggle so that I may experience the growth. It is amazing that you love me enough to grow me into the best me I can be . . . the woman you know I can become, the servant I can become.

When troubles of any kind come your way, consider it an opportunity for great joy. For you know that when your faith is tested, your endurance has a chance to grow.

James 1:2–3

48

Help in Guiding My Children

Father,

I love my children with all my heart and I'm very thankful for them, but parenting is a big responsibility. I'm not just talking about keeping them alive, fed, and dressed. No, there's much more. For example, I want to help my children become strong, independent-thinking humans who do not blindly follow popular opinion or submit to peer pressure. I want them to know it's okay to think for themselves and to be willing to stand up for their beliefs, even if their friends don't like it.

But Father, it's hard to teach them that. It's even hard for me to do those things sometimes. I want them to have discernment and wisdom, balanced with courage and kindness. Guide me in how much freedom to allow them, how much space to give them. Show me how much advice to offer, especially when it isn't asked for. Give me courage to trust them when they've shown they deserve my trust and strength to enforce guidelines when they haven't earned it. I pray that they will see my love in all I say and do . . . even when I mess up. I pray they will love you, follow you, and serve you. I earnestly pray that you will become the guiding force in their lives—their true north.

Start children off on the way they should go, and even when they are old they will not turn from it.

Proverbs 22:6 NIV

49

Guarding My Words

Father,

I confess that I am undisciplined in the words I speak. I say things to others that would crush me if they were spoken to me. I confess that I speak words of judgment and criticism. Words that could certainly harm reputations and ultimately destroy relationships. I'm sorry for my hurtful words. I also confess to you that I speak pious words of godly obedience and honor toward you, but those words are not supported by my own behavior. They are lies I speak to make myself look better.

Lord, I'm sorry for my laziness in guarding my words. I confess and repent of this behavior. My heart's deep desire is to speak and live in a way that conveys your love for others. But I haven't been doing that. I'm sorry. I ask you to help me be more conscious of the words I speak. Help me think before speaking—to my family and to others.

Lord, keep this foremost in my mind. Remind me that the words I speak often reflect my heart. I recognize that I need to align my heart with you in obedience to you and love for you and others. Help me to be honest in what I say. Help me be aware of how my words land on others' hearts and how those words reflect on you.

Stay clear of pious talk that is only talk. Words are not mere words, you know. If they're not backed by a godly life, they accumulate as poison in the soul.

2 Timothy 2:16–17 The Message

50

Leaning on Jesus

Father,

Sometimes life is plain old hard. Situations, problems, and life changes are painful, even when they eventually lead to good things. I understand that the process of my faith growing stronger will only happen when I am depending on you and trusting you. Don't get me wrong; I want the growth, but the struggle hurts. My tendency is to ask you to take the pain away . . . to fix the situation and restore calm normality to my life. Honestly, I just want to escape the difficulties.

Yet I realize that the process of becoming more like Jesus must lead me through times when I have nothing left to lean on except you, when all my other support systems are gone, when I just have you. That's when the changes will come in my heart and in my attitude. Father, I don't want a stagnant faith. I do want to grow! What could be better than to have the King of the Universe, the Sovereign Lord of all working in my heart? That's what I want!

So, Lord, give me the strength to endure. Give me the trust to know that you are growing and transforming me into the image of Jesus. That's the goal. It's exactly what I want . . . no matter what.

We all, who with unveiled faces contemplate the Lord's glory, are being transformed into his image with ever-increasing glory, which comes from the Lord, who is the Spirit.

2 Corinthians 3:18 NIV

51

Help Me Be a Godly Grandma

Oh Father,

Thank you for the privilege of being a grandmother. What a joy! I had no idea how much fun grandchildren would be! I love playing with them, singing to them, reading books to them. It's amazing to see my own child's characteristics and appearance come through in these precious grands. The same quizzical look. The teasing grin. Interests in the same things. It feels like my children grew up so fast, but now I get to enjoy the wonders of childhood again through my grands.

Father, help me be a good example to these little ones. Help me be patient and loving (and firm when I need to be). Most of all, help me show them the love of Jesus by how I interact with them, with their parents, and with others. Help me be consistent in showing love, kindness, compassion, and generosity. Remind me that those little eyes are watching and little ears are listening, so I must be honest and sincere in all I say and do. Guard my words from being judgmental or critical.

Oh Lord, I pray for my dear grands to come to know you early, to learn to love you deeply, and to serve you with their whole lives.

Follow God's example, therefore, as dearly loved children and walk in the way of love, just as Christ loved us and gave himself up for us as a fragrant offering and sacrifice to God.

Ephesians 5:1–2 NIV

52

Becoming a Better Me

Father,

I'm amazed by your love. I mean really amazed. You see all the parts of me—the good, the bad, the really ugly—and still you love me. You watch as I ride the waves of life, sometimes honoring you and obeying your Word—sometimes not. There are ups and downs, successes and failures, and still you love me. You always love me. Thank you for your grace. Thank you for your forgiveness. Thank you for second, third, and fiftieth chances to follow and obey you. I love you for all that.

But Father, in the journey to be the me you've made me to be, I have a request . . . help me to become that "better" me. When I lose my temper or sink into selfishness, gossip, judgment . . . failure . . . I beat myself up. I believe I am a disappointment to you (and certainly to myself). Even though I know you forgive me and love me still, I can't seem to get past my own sin. That lack of self-forgiveness holds me back from becoming a better me. Father, help me forgive myself and move on, because that's what you want for me. Help me to love myself, as you do . . . in fact . . . because you do.

There is no room in love for fear. Well-formed love banishes fear. Since fear is crippling, a fearful life—fear of death, fear of judgment —is one not yet fully formed in love.

1 John 4:18 The Message

53

Knowing Christ

Father,

There are many different opinions, interpretations, and even rules about what it looks like to be a Christ follower. I admit that I get confused, sometimes angry, and then just plain old tired. I'm often not proud of how Christians present Christianity to the world. We are too often unforgiving, judgmental, and therefore not loving. We create boxes for people to fit into because the boundaries make us comfortable, even if they aren't scriptural. We set rules instead of allowing you to teach and lead others. I don't think you meant it to be this way.

Father, Colossians 3:3 explains that real life is found in truly knowing Christ. Really knowing him. Studying how he lived. Learning what he said. Behaving the way he behaved. Loving the way he loved. Oh God, help me to know him— really know him—and to pattern my life after him. Then all the questions of what it means to be a Christ follower will be answered. I will be living my life to show others what you are like and how you love. Oh God, I want to focus on that, not on creating boxes for others but only on being like Jesus, loving like Jesus, and sharing Jesus with others.

Your old life is dead. Your new life, which is your real life—even though invisible to spectators—is with Christ in God. He is your life.

Colossians 3:3 The Message

54

Show Me How to Rest in You

Dear God,

I've finally realized that one of the most important things I can ask you is to teach me how to stress less, worry less, be anxious less. I admit that it's taken me a while to understand that, since my natural tendency is to be controlling. I long to learn how to bring my worries and cares to the foot of the cross and just leave them there without grabbing them back to worry over and stress about. I'm good at the bringing to you part but not so much at the leaving them there part.

You have promised to give me rest, but I will never have that if I don't learn how to receive it. Help me learn to trust you and center my thoughts on you instead of the barrage of things attacking my heart. I'm grateful that you offer rest and peace along with your promise that you've got a good handle on all that's happening. But I can't really appreciate or enjoy that rest when I keep my overstressed hands tightly on everything I think I need to control.

I'm tired, Lord. I long for rest. So I ask your Spirit to teach me, guide me, show me how to let go and rest in you.

Jesus said, "Come to me, all of you who are weary and carry heavy burdens, and I will give you rest. Take my yoke upon you. Let me teach you, because I am humble and gentle at heart, and you will find rest for your souls."

Matthew 11:28–29

55

Live in Love

Father God,

In this ever-widening, changing world we don't always speak in ways that show our love for you and others. It's hard to stay true to our faith and morals and yet speak in ways that will draw people to you instead of pushing them away. Father, I want to show your love to all I interact with. Thankfully, you don't change and your Word doesn't change. Truth is truth. But how I live in our quickly changing world, well, that may need to change. Maybe what worked twenty-five or fifty years ago needs to be adjusted in today's world.

Father, help me stay true to you and model the love that Jesus lived. To love without concern about another person's status or sin or even agreement with what I believe. To love but still clearly declare my devotion to you and your Word. I pray that my love would help bring them into an awareness of you and a desire to know you and live with you and for you. It's hard sometimes, yes, but by the power of your Spirit guiding my thoughts, my actions, my words, it can be done. And as I honestly live in love, all those around me, friends and strangers, will see it. Praise you, Father—they will feel it.

A new commandment I give to you, that you love one another: just as I have loved you, you also are to love one another.

John 13:34 ESV

56

My Work for Jesus

Oh God,

What can I possibly offer you? I'm just one woman. I'm busy all day with things (that I believe are important), and by evening . . . I'm tired. I want to have a role in your work, I want to make a difference for your kingdom, but . . . I'm just one woman.

However, when I read how Jesus lived and what he did here on earth, I see that women were important to him. He spent a lot of time with women—forgiving them, saving them, healing them, loving them. So that tells me I do matter to you. It tells me that my work for you right now is important, even if it is to simply love my neighbors and help wherever I see a need.

I know that my *real* work for you is to bring Jesus into the lives of those I meet. I can do that by caring for my coworkers, loving people who aren't easy to love, and serving others. What an honor that is. What can I offer you? My heart. My life. My words. Being a part of your work is accomplished in the moment-by-moment attitudes and actions of . . . just one woman.

Dear friends, let us continue to love one another, for love comes from God. Anyone who loves is a child of God and knows God.

1 John 4:7

57

Trusting God for Healing

Loving Father and Great Physician,

My heart is heavy for my loved one who is suffering with serious health problems. I come to you because of your great love and concern for your children. I know you love this dear one even more than I do. So I ask you to heal her. Father, wrap your loving arms around her. Hold her close. Help her to rest in your embrace. Help her to have real peace because of your love and compassion. Help her to know your plan is *for* her good.

You know, Lord, that my desire is for you to totally heal her body. I love her and long for her presence in my life for years to come. I know I don't need to point out what a blessing she is to so many people. You know that already. You know that her heart belongs to you and that she loves you very much. I'm going to say something that's hard to say . . . I trust you with her life. I trust you to carry out your plan, and I know that whatever happens is what you've chosen for her and therefore what's best for her.

Be gentle with her, loving Father. Flood her heart with the knowledge and experience of your presence and your love.

Give thanks to the God of gods,
for his steadfast love endures forever.

Psalm 136:2 ESV

58

Healing
for Us All

Oh Lord,

Our world is in such a mess. I'm afraid for us.
I'm heartbroken for us. Lord, I pray for unity
in our world . . . especially among Christians.
People should be able to see we are Christians
by our love. I pray that we would put aside the
differences we have and that we would come
together to be your witnesses in this broken
world. I pray that we would join hands and
serve those who need serving—even (especially) those who are so different from us. May

we in Christian love help those who need help. May we work together to serve those whose lands are torn apart by wars, those who have so little left and who fear for their lives every day.

Father, help our world leaders build relationships with other countries based on respect. Remind your people that we must reach out to those who have so little, need so much, and are so often crippled by famine, drought, and war.

Break our hearts for what breaks yours. Father, break *my* heart for what breaks yours. Help us put those broken hearts into action.

"Lord, when did we ever see you hungry and feed you? Or thirsty and give you something to drink? Or a stranger and show you hospitality? Or naked and give you clothing? When did we ever see you sick or in prison and visit you?"

And the King will say, "I tell you the truth, when you did it to one of the least of these my brothers and sisters, you were doing it to me!"

Matthew 25:37–40

59

Keeping Up Appearances

Father,

I confess that I try to look like I have life all together. I know the right words to say, the good ministries to serve in, the behavior that makes me look good to others. But the truth is that in my heart I'm struggling. Oh God, I struggle with uncertainties. I have questions. I have fears. I worry. I fret. I doubt . . . all things that I don't think Christians are supposed to do. I'm supposed to trust you in all things, but sometimes I don't. I'm supposed to be loving and kind, but sometimes I'm not. I'm guilty of putting on the mask of Christianity, but beneath that mask is a struggling believer.

Why do I work so hard to put up a good front? Simple answer: I'm keeping up appearances. Because what if others should think less of me? What if I disappoint them?

Oh God, all that matters is what you think. I know you see my confusion and doubt, and you don't think less of me. You understand and you care. You know that it's through my questions and doubts that I learn. Thank you for the journey and for understanding how I'm traveling on it. Help me, Father, to take off the mask and just be real.

I am sure of this, that he who began a good work in you will bring it to completion at the day of Jesus Christ.

Philippians 1:6 ESV

60

Grateful for God's Love

Loving God,

I am incredibly grateful for your merciful, gracious love. I do my best to be aware of that love both in the small things of my life and in the big things. Of course, I feel it in the constant presence of blessings I enjoy—like the warmth of sunshine, beauty of flowers, clear, blue skies, precious family, friends, music, good books. These are things I can easily take for granted because some of them seem so, I don't know, normal? But then I see your love in majestic ways as well, as in forgiving my sins . . . over and over. I'm very grateful for that.

I see your love in your grace to give me many opportunities to learn and grow, and you never ever give up on me. I see it in your answers to my prayers. I see it in salvation that gives me the promise of eternity with you and that is never taken away. Your love provides prayer, which gives me a way to tell you what I'm feeling and longing for and dreaming of. And I know that you hear me . . . and you care. You show your love in so very many ways, and I feel so very, very blessed. Thank you.

But you, O Lord,
*   are a God of compassion and mercy,*
slow to get angry
*   and filled with unfailing love and*
*   faithfulness.*

Psalm 86:15

61

Resisting the Lies

Dear God,

I'm succumbing to Satan's lies. I need your help letting go of his reminders of failures in my past. He builds more lies on top of the lies I've told myself. He works hard to keep me pressed down, inhibited, feeling useless, and all these things make me feel "less than." Those lies haunt my thoughts, keep me awake, make me afraid to step up or step out.

I need a fresh start. I confess my failures to you and ask your forgiveness for my words and my actions that have hurt others in any way. Guide me by your Spirit to know when I need to reach out and apologize to those I've hurt or when it's best to just let it go.

Help me stop believing the lies that Satan constantly feeds me. He knows the places in my heart where I'm unsure and insecure, and that's where he attacks. His lies are not true, and yet I've accepted them as truth for years, and they have shackled me and kept me from living into the adventure you have planned for my life. I want to let go of the lies and enjoy the adventure.

So let God work his will in you. Yell a loud no to the Devil and watch him make himself scarce. Say a quiet yes to God and he'll be there in no time. Quit dabbling in sin. Purify your inner life. Quit playing the field. Hit bottom, and cry your eyes out. The fun and games are over. Get serious, really serious. Get down on your knees before the Master; it's the only way you'll get on your feet.

James 4:7–10 The Message

62

Thankful for Encouragement

Gracious Father,

I am grateful to have been blessed with mentors, friends, and family members who love you and who continually model lives of serving and honoring you. I know they pray diligently for me, and I am grateful for those prayers. I have no doubt that it's because of their prayers that I've been protected more times than I can imagine. I know many of them pray for me every day. These precious ones have supported me and still enthusiastically encourage me to go for my dreams, to be strong, to not be fearful of problems, and to take risks. They've always been there when I've turned to them. Their support, courage, and love have given me strength many times in my life.

Father, please bless these dear ones with good health. Protect them. Guide them. Watch over them and fill their days with purpose and meaning. Help them know they can call on me when they have needs. Life is busy, and I don't see them as often as I would like, but I love them very much. Help them know that their example has taught me to be a mentor, friend, and encourager to others. I am who I am because of their lives. Thank you for them.

Let us think of ways to motivate one another to acts of love and good works.

Hebrews 10:24

63

Precious Promises

Dear Lord,

Thank you for your Word. Thank you for the beauty of its message . . . your message. Studying it prepares me not just to know you but to learn how to live for you moment by moment. It teaches me to be the woman you created me to be. Even on my darkest days, the love poured out from your Word keeps me on my knees worshiping you.

Thank you for the Old Testament stories of your dealings with your people . . . even when the situations were difficult and you had to show your strength, justice, and an insistence on their obedience. That teaches me a lot. Thank you for the stories of how Jesus lived and taught. I enjoy reading of his love and care for people. His heart shines through so clearly. Thank you for the glimpses into what is to come. I'll admit that some things are frightening, but your Word assures me that I am yours and promises that whatever happens you are with me. It gives me the promise of eternity with you! That gives me joy.

Each time I read your Word it speaks to me. I know it's you telling me just what I need to know for that day. Your Word is my lifeline to you.

All Scripture is inspired by God and beneficial for teaching, for rebuke, for correction, for training in righteousness; so that the man or woman of God may be fully capable, equipped for every good work.

2 Timothy 3:16–17 NASB

64

Beautiful, Amazing Grace

My precious Lord,

Grace. Grace is an amazing, wonderful thing, though I confess that I don't understand it. I cannot grasp the depth of how important grace is to my daily life and to my future. I couldn't even be talking to you right now if it were not for your grace. I wouldn't be able to know you if it were not for your grace. I wouldn't have faced my sinfulness or even known I needed your grace if it were not for your grace. Father, I would have no peace in my life at all if it were not for your grace. There would be no one to trust for guidance and direction in my life.

Once I faced my sins—I mean really faced the fact that I am a sinner—your grace became a reality, providing a way to know you and receive forgiveness for my sins. I don't deserve even a second glance from you. I don't deserve anything at all from you. That's a difficult thing for a woman in this culture to admit. I do admit it though. It is by grace that you look at me without seeing the stains and filth of my sin. Your grace means you see a beautiful me . . . the me I am because of your grace.

God saved you by his grace when you believed. And you can't take credit for this; it is a gift from God. Salvation is not a reward for the good things we have done, so none of us can boast about it.

Ephesians 2:8–9

65

Lord, I Need Your Peace

Lord,

I need peace. I need real, deep peace. My mind and heart are swirling like tornadoes. I'm so worried. I can't think about anything else. I can't even sleep. I know you love me. I know you want to help me. I know you're waiting on me to come to you. So I bring my burden, my concern, my worry to you. You know what's going on. I don't have to spell it out for you. You saw the situation before it ever became my reality. Oh God, you know I can't face this without you. I don't know what to do. I can't handle the uncertainty, pressure, or pain.

Please fill me with your strength, Lord. Comfort my heart with the steady assurance that you're with me and you've got this. Fill me with your peace. I want to honestly trust that even in this chaos and darkness, you have things under control. I want to trust that your plan is being worked out. I understand that it may not be what I want, but I'm slowly learning to trust your plan more than mine.

I pray, Lord, for the submissive courage to let go of my worry and simply, wholly trust you. Only then will I have the peace I long for.

Commit your way to the LORD;
trust in him, and he will act.
Psalm 37:5 ESV

66

Submitting to My Lord

Lord,

I so easily call you that. Lord . . . but do I really even understand what that word means? Have I actually thought about how it defines the role you should have in my life? Submitting to you as Lord of my life goes deeper than recognizing you as my Savior, as important as that first step is. Oh God, I am humbled, grateful, and blessed to acknowledge you as my Savior, who paid the price for my sin, forgives my sinful acts and thoughts, and cleanses my heart. You saved me from an eternity separated from you. Being saved means I have the promise of heaven! But recognizing you as Lord means so much more.

How do I allow you lordship in my life? I do so by submitting to your authority, your leadership, and your will. I long to serve you and to become the woman you want me to be. More of you . . . less of me. The possibilities in that excite me! Lordship means I give you control of my life—"not my will but thine"—knowing that you, my Lord, want good things for me . . . in fact, the very best for me. Thank you, my precious Lord.

I have been crucified with Christ and I no longer live, but Christ lives in me. The life I now live in the body, I live by faith in the Son of God, who loved me and gave himself for me.

Galatians 2:20 NIV

67

Confidence in God's Plan

Dear Lord Jesus,

What a blessing it is that I can have complete confidence in you. I have confidence because I know you are trustworthy and that you always keep your promises. You have proven that over and over through the evidence seen in Scripture and certainly in my own life. I can trust that you have a wonderful plan for my life and that you are working that plan out day by day, moment by moment—even when I can't see how things can possibly turn out well, I have confidence in you. I trust that your ways are better than anything I might plan for myself. After all, I look at the immediate and want instant gratification, peace, or success. But thankfully, you see a much bigger picture and have higher aspirations for me than I have for myself. I know that even when the process of growing is difficult or painful, it is for my good because it will bring me to a place of stronger faith, deeper trust, and grow me to be more like Jesus. Growing pains are never easy but always worthwhile.

Thank you, Father, for consistently being true to your character. Because of who you are I have complete confidence in you and your plans for me.

God has given both his promise and his oath. These two things are unchangeable because it is impossible for God to lie. Therefore, we who have fled to him for refuge can have great confidence as we hold to the hope that lies before us.

Hebrews 6:18

68

God Uses Ordinary People

Oh God,

Sometimes I feel like I'm drowning in the critical, negative voice in my head. That voice constantly reminds me that I'm no one special—just plain old ordinary me. It tells me that I'm never going to do great things for you. It reminds me that sometimes I struggle to even be a kind, decent human.

Oh Lord, help me remember that you didn't choose superheroes to lead your people or teach others. You chose ordinary people and empowered them with your strength, courage, wisdom, and love. Yes, many of them did great things for you, but not by their own power . . . it was all you.

You have a plan and purpose for me too, Lord. I know you do. Maybe I'll "be Jesus" to only one person. Maybe I'll have a broader in fluence. One person or thousands—it doesn't matter. Your plan for me is best. I just ask you to help me push away the negative self-talk and concentrate on knowing you and obeying you one moment at a time. Help me to consistently be available to follow your guidance and be of use to you. Help me remember this: I have value because you value me!

Don't copy the behavior and customs of this world, but let God transform you into a new person by changing the way you think. Then you will learn to know God's will for you, which is good and pleasing and perfect.

Romans 12:2

69

Remembering God Is God

Father,

Thank you for lighting a passion in my soul. Thank you for opening my heart to see problems and needs around me and then planting a desire in my soul to help. I care deeply about others, and I want to be useful to your work by helping others know how much you love them. But Father, help me remember that solving the problems of the world does not rest on my shoulders. While I do care, I realize that I'm not in control—you are. You are God. I am not.

My wish to solve every problem I encounter reflects my desire to have a meaningful part of your work here. But I confess that I get discouraged when I try and it seems like nothing changes. So I ask you, Father, to rein in my discouragement and help me remember to bathe every action, every decision in prayer and then trust you with the outcome. I pray for you to show me my part in the work. Show me how to take things a step at a time. Keep me from discouragement but give me persistence. Help me, Father, to simply be available to you and not try to outrun you to do your work.

All the world from east to west
will know there is no other God.
I am the LORD, and there is no other.
I create the light and make the
darkness.
I send good times and bad times.
I, the LORD, am the one who does
these things.

Isaiah 45:6–7

70

You Are
My Everything

Oh God,

You are everything to me. Because of you I know peace, which means I can know rest. Because of you I have calm that comes from trusting you. Because of you I can take deep, invigorating, life-giving breaths regardless of what chaos surrounds me. These things are possible only because of your presence in my life.

When I'm afraid, I call on you for help and you give me peace. When I'm overwhelmed, I call on you and you give me rest. When life is chaotic, I call on you and you give me calm.

God, you give my life meaning. You guide my way by lighting the path when I see only darkness. Of course, my life isn't problem-free, but that's because you love me enough to grow me through the trust and faith that struggles bring. You bless me with life, relationships, encouragement, and opportunities. You give my life purpose as I become more like Jesus and seek to serve you by loving others.

Thank you for your love, freely given. Thank you for your forgiveness, even though it's undeserved. Thank you for daily blessings that sometimes surprise me enough to take my breath away. You are so good to me. You are my everything.

You, LORD, are my shepherd.
I will never be in need.
You let me rest in fields of green grass.
You lead me to streams of peaceful water,
and you refresh my life.

Psalm 23:1–3 CEV

71

Majestic Miracles

Oh God,

You are the God of miracles, so I am boldly asking for a miracle. This current situation in my life is overwhelming. God, it feels hopeless, so I'm not asking for just any old miracle, I'm asking for a majestic miracle. Majestic—I mean a miracle so amazing that everyone stands amazed, jaws dropped open, eyes wide with wonder because we all know that what happened had to come from you and only you. There can be no other explanation. Your miracle will be too amazing to have been provided by a mere human.

I know I'm asking a lot, but you said that I can ask anything in faith, believing you will answer. So, I'm asking. My loving God, I will, of course, accept whatever answer you give. You know what I want you to do, but you know what's best for all of us. So, Lord, even if you don't give the miracle I want, I will thank you for your answer and know that you love all the people involved . . . even more than I do. Still I pray, oh God of majestic miracles, please amaze us with your power and love.

I am the LORD, the God of all mankind. Is anything too hard for me?

Jeremiah 32:27 NIV

72

Grow My Passion for You

Father,

This isn't easy to admit, but . . . I confess that I too easily slide into faith complacency. I don't mean to, of course, but the habits I've built, which were actually meant to grow my faith stronger, have instead dulled my passions simply by their familiarity. My passion for being in your presence grows dim. My desire to spend time reading Scripture weakens. I begin drifting along in my life, going through the motions of faith. Father, I believe Satan uses this tactic to keep me from effectively living and working for you. He encourages me to slip away from you without even realizing it's happening.

I don't want this apathy to continue, so I ask for your help to stop this from happening. I ask you, Lord, to wake me up from complacency. I ask for renewed passion to grip my heart, pulling me to you, making me hunger to be in your presence and to sink deep into your Word. Oh God, remind me how very much you love me! I long to feel alive in you! Keep me from the temptation to get lazy about my life with you. Keep in the forefront of my heart that the days are short and life in you is the most important thing.

Be very careful, then, how you live—not as unwise but as wise, making the most of every opportunity, because the days are evil.

Ephesians 5:15–16 NIV

73

Prodigal Returnings

Father,

I want to thank you for never giving up on me. There's wonderful security in the truth that you will not let me go. I may drift away at times, but you never drift from me. Satan tries to pull me away from you, and sometimes he is successful for a moment. But I always come back to you because with you is where I want to be. In the loud, chaotic cacophony of this world I listen for your voice. I hear it in my heart and mind. Sometimes I may get confused by a voice that calls more loudly. Sometimes I even deliberately ignore your voice. I'm always sorry for that and grateful to be able to humbly come back to you—hopefully having learned a lesson to keep me from making the same mistake again.

Your love, wisdom, patience, forgiveness, grace, and promise of eternity with you are incredible gifts to me. I'm so blessed, so grateful, so amazed that you will not let anyone or anything snatch me from you. When I fall away, I always come back to you because close to you is where I want to be.

My sheep know my voice, and I know them. They follow me, and I give them eternal life, so that they will never be lost. No one can snatch them out of my hand.

John 10:27–28 CEV

74

God's Care

Loving Father,

You take such good care of me. I have all I need, even if not all I want. I'm thankful that you don't shame me for asking for what I want or telling you what I think I need. You always hear me, and you care about how I feel. Father, I'm learning (perhaps more slowly than I should be) that I have all I need, and that's absolutely enough. Your generous provisions of grace and forgiveness show me the enormity of your love.

It's taken a while, but I'm learning that the material things I ask you for are wants, not needs, and while sometimes you give them, sometimes you don't. I'm learning that the things I ask you to do for me and for those I love are not always the best things for us in the big picture of life, and you know that. I know that you answer my requests as you do because you see the implications for me spiritually and how my requests will impact the future me.

Thank you for loving so strongly that you say "no" or "not right now." Thank you for helping me learn to be content with life. I am content in you and because of you.

Not that I am speaking of being in need, for I have learned in whatever situation I am to be content. I know how to be brought low, and I know how to abound. In any and every circumstance, I have learned the secret of facing plenty and hunger, abundance and need.

Philippians 4:11–12 ESV

75

Risk-Taking Faith

Oh Father,

You know I'm not a brave woman. I'm not comfortable taking chances. I'm fearful of making mistakes. I'm scared of being hurt. I obey rules. Let's face it . . . I'm a "stay within the lines" kind of person. But God, I don't want to live a scaredy-cat life. I don't want to be so fearful that I miss being part of something adventurous and exciting. I don't want to come to the end of my life and find I haven't lived.

Help me be willing to take risks—even knowing I might fail. To have new experiences in serving you, I have to be brave enough to try new things . . . scary things. If I fail then I fail. But sometimes, with your guidance and direction, I won't fail. You certainly give me opportunities to get out of my comfort zone. Oh God, give me courage to follow your leading, to step out in faith, to not be afraid. I want to have the kind of faith that trusts you enough to give me new experiences. I want to be useful to you in ways I've never imagined. I want to be brave! I want to have a risk-taking faith because I have a trustworthy God! What fun we'll have! Let the adventures begin!

Haven't I commanded you? Strength! Courage! Don't be timid; don't get discouraged. God, your God, is with you every step you take.

Joshua 1:9 The Message

76

Trusting Till the End

Dear Father,

The privilege of being able to pray to you simply blows my mind. I'm grateful that you invite me to talk with you. You're always eager for conversation with me. You listen . . . no wait, you don't just listen . . . you *hear* me. You actually want to know what I care about.

So I prayed and laid bare the desires of my heart to you. I believed you would answer, and you did. But the answer was not what I wanted. That hurt. I'll be honest, I struggled with it for a while. However, I eventually got my thoughts straight, and here's where I landed: It's true that the answer you gave to the situation was not what I hoped for. But deep in my heart (buried beneath my "wants") I honestly trust and believe that you will always do what's best. Even though I can't see the good in the moment, I believe you're working out your good plan. You see a much bigger picture of the future than I can imagine. Because I know this to be true, I trust that in the end everything will be all right. If things are not all right, then I know it isn't yet the end

We know that God causes everything to work together for the good of those who love God and are called according to his purpose for them.

Romans 8:28

77

Encouraging Others

My loving Father,

I'm going to be honest here. I usually feel like I am in pretty good shape when it comes to being a good Christian woman. I even look around at others and silently think, "Well, I'm doing better than she is." Or, "At least I don't make choices like he does." Whew. Just by admitting those thoughts I recognize how far away from being a "good Christian woman" I am. What I have come to realize, God, is that where I let my thoughts settle says a lot about my faith and the health of my walk with you. Building myself up at the expense of or by judging others is not a loving thing to do. It's not even Christian. Their lives are between them and you . . . not me!

I'm sorry, God, that I am (secretly) self-focused and even self-worshiping sometimes. My pride about what a good person I think I am is a sin. Please forgive me. Help me do better. Help me *be* better. Show me how to be honestly, truly humble. Help me learn to lift others up instead of comparing myself to them or judging them. Help me develop a heart that cheerleads for others, encouraging them to become the best they can be with no envy or comparison on my part—just joyous celebration for them!

Don't push your way to the front; don't sweet talk your way to the top. Put yourself aside, and help others get ahead. Don't be obsessed with getting your own advantage. Forget yourselves long enough to lend a helping hand.

Philippians 2:3–4 The Message

78

The Waste of Worry

Oh Father,

If worry and anxiety were spiritual gifts, I'd be a spiritual giant! I spend so much energy worrying about what might happen . . . could happen . . . might not happen . . . and even what *did* happen. None of which I can control! I know my worry can't change a thing, but that doesn't slow it down much. I even lie awake worrying. I can't eat, or worse, I eat too much (of the wrong foods!). I don't enjoy the beauty around me or the people around me, and they don't enjoy me because I'm so unpleasantly anxious.

Oh Father, I want to stop. I want to trust you with every aspect of my life. I want to be able to bring my worries and fears to you and just leave them with you because I know you can and will handle them. I ask your help when I obsess about something. Help me remember that you have things under control . . . and you don't need my help. Help me remember that most of the things I worry about will never actually happen anyway. I'm tired of worrying. I know you're tired of my worry too and that you'll help me.

God cares for you, so turn all your worries over to him.

1 Peter 5:7 CEV

79

A Cord of
Three Strands

Father,

I am a people person. Of course, I need my alone time. In fact, I value it. But I gain energy, joy, and encouragement from being with people. Thank you for the people you've put in my life who care enough to watch out for me, help me, encourage me, and challenge me. There are some who hold me accountable for choices I make. There are some who will challenge me regarding words I speak and attitudes I hold. There are those who keep me from wandering away from the path of serving and obeying you. I appreciate the friend who calls me out when I'm not being true to myself or to who you've called me to be. I'm thankful that each of these friends love me enough to take the risk of challenging me. I'm stronger because of them. I'm braver because of them. I'm confident because of them. Their concern helps me fight off temptation, and they help me stay close to you. These friends are a gift from you. The three of us—me, my friends, and you—we can stand against anything.

A person standing alone can be attacked and defeated, but two can stand back-to-back and conquer. Three are even better, for a triple-braided cord is not easily broken.

Ecclesiastes 4:12

80

The Father's Love Song

Oh God,

I am totally amazed by your love, Lord. The very word *love* defines you ("God is love," 1 John 4:8). Oh God, just reading the words in Scripture that tell me how much you love me is heartwarming and encouraging. But to read that you actually sing love songs over me is just mind-blowing. What a beautiful thought—I have my very own God-created love song!

What's amazing to me is that you keep loving me when I fail you so often. That makes your beautiful love songs even more humbling. I can't begin to fathom the width and depth of your love.

Your Word tells me over and over that you love me more than I can imagine and in ways I can't possibly understand. You love me so much that you choose to live in me. Your sacrificial love saves me. Your love gives me forgiveness. You care for me and provide for me. You protect me, guide me, and teach me. And then . . . you sing my song to me when I need to hear it. You sing a song to my heart that tells me of your amazing love. Thank you for your love.

The LORD your God is living among you.
He is a mighty savior.
He will take delight in you with gladness.
With his love, he will calm all your fears.
He will rejoice over you with joyful songs.

                                  Zephaniah 3:17

81

Blessed Guidance

My precious Lord,

I am very grateful that you allow me the freedom to make my own choices and decisions. I'm even more grateful that you pay attention to the ones I make. I am often so confident that I know what I'm doing, and I confess that I'm certainly a strong-willed, stubborn woman. Too often I barrel ahead in life without even a thought of asking your guidance. Of course, once my decisions are made, I quite willingly ask you to bless them.

I'm so grateful that when I do stop and talk to you before rushing forward, your guidance is always given freely. Even though I've so often rushed ahead of you, you still guide me as to where to go and what to do. If I make a decision that isn't good, you close that door and then redirect me. I just know that if I do ask your guidance and then pay attention, you will keep me from wandering too far off the right path.

So please, Lord, forgive my stubbornness, guide my thoughts and ideas, and direct my steps. Thank you for being my GPS. I know I can trust your guidance.

Your own ears will hear him.
Right behind you a voice will say,
"This is the way you should go,"
whether to the right or to the left.

Isaiah 30:21

82

Standing for Christ

Father,

Your followers are openly criticized for our faith, morals, beliefs, and attitudes. Yes, sometimes the criticisms are justified because some of us behave badly and fail to show love to those who disagree with us. But often the anger and criticism are not fair. I know I should be willing to take a stand (with love and grace) and face any ugliness that's thrown at me. After all, I know what my heart feels toward you and toward others, and I know how you feel about me.

But sometimes I'm anxious and I just want to be quiet about my faith because I fear the ridicule, sarcasm, or anger. Yet I know that you are watching out for me. You will protect me. With you on my side I shouldn't fear anything or anyone.

Oh God, help me remember that you're with me. When I want to shrink into the shadows, remind me that you will stand with me when I stand for you. Remind me that you will give me the words to say (or not say) when my faith in you is challenged. You will love others through my attitudes, words, and actions—even those who don't yet know that you love them. You are on my side, and that's all that matters!

What can we say about all this? If God is on our side, can anyone be against us?

Romans 8:31 CEV

83

Your Word Is My Lifeline

Father,

Each time I read your Word you speak to me in a new way. You awaken my heart to the beauty of your love and the depth of your desire to be close with me. I'm thankful for the various translations that speak to me in different ways at different times and in different situations. I'm grateful that you always know exactly what I need to hear. When I'm going through difficult things, you bring your words of strength, guidance, and love alive in my soul. When I need guidance, your words of wisdom shine forth.

Thank you, Father, for guiding my life through your Word. Thank you for knowing the struggles I will face, even before I know, and giving wisdom through your Word. Thank you for Scripture's challenges to stay close to you and to be obedient to you. Thank you that through your Word I learn how to become the woman you have planned for me to be. Your Word trains me in knowing you more deeply and serving you humbly and willingly. It challenges me to love you with all my heart. It instructs me to love others sacrificially. Thank you that as I read, meditate, and study your Word it becomes more precious to me. Scripture is my lifeline to you!

Every part of Scripture is God-breathed and useful one way or another—showing us truth, exposing our rebellion, correcting our mistakes, training us to live God's way. Through the Word we are put together and shaped up for the tasks God has for us.

2 Timothy 3:16–17 The Message

84

An Undivided Heart

Lord,

I understand that I cannot be halfhearted in my desire to know you. I can't just call on you when I want something from you or when I want to ask you to fix something or provide something with no other pursuit of a relationship with you. I can't treat you like you're just there to do what I want.

Seeking you with *all* my heart means that my desires and my thoughts should always be centered on you. My goal must be to know you deeply and personally, to understand who you are and what you want for me and from me. My desire must be to obey you according to the knowledge I have and then to increase that knowledge so I learn how to obey you more. My purpose is to serve you in any way that you direct me, and my humble obedience is my response to you.

Oh God, I want that so much! All my heart, oh Lord. I want all my heart to be yours. I do not want to allow it to be divided between you and something else. If I allow that to happen, I will not fully find you, know you, and love you. Oh God, protect me from a divided heart so that I may know the true fullness of an amazing life that has you at the center.

You will seek me and find me when you seek me with all your heart.

Jeremiah 29:13 NIV

85

Loving Others

Father,

I've messed up. I've been putting a lot of emphasis on things other than love. I've arrogantly insisted that everyone believe like I believe and do what I say is right. I guess I want us to all be the same. And if people can't do that, well, they become the "them" to my "us," and that creates a division between us. That means if I do try to love them, my love is actually conditional on them believing and behaving just as I do.

Oh God, I don't want to be like this. I don't want my love to be conditional. I want to love as Jesus instructed me to love . . . to love as he does. I need to allow others to make their own choices about the lives they lead. Their choices are between them and you. It is not for me to judge them. Lord, help me to love them . . . just to love them.

Of course, I can lovingly challenge Christian brothers and sisters who are drifting from you. I get that. But thinking about people who don't know you . . . help me to love them first, without judgment . . . love them the way you do so they can see and feel your love through me. Honestly. Sincerely. Love is the greatest.

Three things will last forever—faith, hope, and love—and the greatest of these is love.

1 Corinthians 13:13

86

Pray, Holy Spirit

Oh God,

My heart is aching more than I've ever known. I'm scared. I'm anxious. I'm confused. I'm hurting for people I love very much. I need to talk with you and tell you how I feel, but Father, I don't even know how to pray about this. I don't know what to say. I have no idea what the best way to resolve this might be. The situation is layered, and while I love all the people involved, I realize that what seems best for one person could really destroy another person. I don't know what the best outcome is, so I don't even know what to say.

Father, I ask your Holy Spirit to pray for this as you have said he will. I ask that he pray for your will, for your guidance, for your love to shine brightly in this. I pray for your comfort for every person involved. I know each one is confused and hurting too. Father, you know what's best for all. Hear your Spirit's prayer, Father. Hear his pleas for these dear ones. Work out your loving will in each heart. Take care of tender hearts through these difficult times. Please, Father. Please. May these precious loved ones know that your hand is in whatever happens.

The Holy Spirit helps us in our weakness. For example, we don't know what God wants us to pray for. But the Holy Spirit prays for us with groanings that cannot be expressed in words. And the Father who knows all hearts knows what the Spirit is saying, for the Spirit pleads for us believers in harmony with God's own will.

Romans 8:26–27

87

No Matter What

Father,

I know that you won't prevent me from facing difficult times. The reason is that I learn from those hard things. I think about the Hebrews being rescued from Egypt only to be led into the wilderness. The wilderness gave them opportunities to trust, learn, and see your provision. They were *never* alone on that journey. You led them, walked with them, worked with them every step of the way.

Similarly, as I face struggles and challenges, I find strength from you to get through them. I learn about you and how to trust you to be with me in the pain and the struggles. You have promised to keep me safe from the dangers and problems life brings. That doesn't mean things won't hurt—sometimes I hurt a lot. The pain is sometimes from choices I make and sometimes it's from things I have no control over. But I don't have to face hard times alone because you promised to always be with me.

Father, hold me close to you. Help me keep my focus on you! Keep me from trying to control things on my own. Keep me from turning away from you. The greatest blessing is knowing you are with me no matter what.

The LORD will protect you
and keep you safe
from all dangers.
The LORD will protect you
now and always
wherever you go.
    Psalm 121:7–8 CEV

88

Your Incredible Power

Father,

Sometimes in my mind I kind of gloss over how powerful you are. There's no doubt that I really have no grasp of your incredible power or that it is available to me through you. If I did I wouldn't try to do things on my own so often. I wouldn't fret and agonize over things when all I actually need to do is bring them to you and leave them there.

Your power, God, is greater than I can conceive. I mean, you made all there is. You control the ocean waves, storms, volcanoes, earthquakes, sun, moon, and stars, and still you know every bird that flies, and you know how many hairs are on my head. You know the things I do, the words I say, and the thoughts I have and those of every person on earth. Not only do you know these things, but your power can guide my thoughts, words, actions . . . if I will just listen to you. Your power can turn my steps to the right when there is danger to the left. Your power can stop me from hurting someone because of my own pride or selfishness. Your power is all I need. Thank you for loving me and offering your power. Help me, Father, to submit to you so I can know the incredible greatness of your power.

I also pray that you will understand the incredible greatness of God's power for us who believe him. This is the same mighty power that raised Christ from the dead and seated him in the place of honor at God's right hand in the heavenly realms.

Ephesians 1:19–20

89

Take Me Down a Notch

Dear God,

I'm grateful for the people who walk through life with me. I need them. I appreciate them even when I don't like how they push me hard and challenge me in uncomfortable ways. I'm aware that just as they give me support, encouragement, friendship, laughter, fun, and shared tears, I also need to be available to do that for others. We're all on this planet to help each other.

But I'm going to be honest here—sometimes there are people around me who I just don't want to help . . . for different reasons. Mostly it's because I am critical and judgmental of their choices or I (wrongly) feel I'm above helping some people. Oh God, I can be arrogant. I'm not proud of that. It's humbling to admit that I am.

Lord, I ask you to take me down a notch when necessary. Help me become more willing to reach out to anyone you put in my path who needs help—without choosing only those I deem worthy of my precious time. Oh Lord, don't let me get stuck in the arrogance of feeling more important than others. In my heart I know I'm not more important, but still I get caught there sometimes. Forgive me. Teach me. Help me.

Share each other's burdens, and in this way obey the law of Christ. If you think you are too important to help someone, you are only fooling yourself. You are not that important.

Galatians 6:2–3

90

Just Live like Jesus

Dear Lord,

It sounds simple . . . just live like Jesus. Treat people the way he did, love like he did, help like he did. It should be simple, but it's not. I get uncomfortable around people whose lives are so different from mine. I shy away from those who don't speak my language. I'm fearful of people who lead a rougher life than I do. I guess I've created boundaries of loving and helping only those inside the lines that I'm comfortable with. Often those boundaries seem to leave

Jesus on the outside. But Father, how will those on the outside of my comfort zone hear about you or know your love and care if I don't reach out to them?

I love you, and I long to honor you by how I live. I long to serve you by serving any you bring into my path. I will study Jesus's life. I will make the effort to live as he did. Give me the courage to honor you by how I receive others, how I serve and love others. To "be Jesus" to others I have to be willing to be around them, talk with them, know them. Father, you love them, and I can be the bridge for them to know you. Give me the opportunities and the courage, and I will obey.

Anyone who claims to be intimate with God ought to live the same kind of life Jesus lived.

1 John 2:6 The Message

91

The Right Priorities

Father,

I suppose it's the culture I live in or the pressures I succumb to, but my life is crazy busy. At least, I blame the culture and pressures. But I don't like the busyness. I don't know how to stop it. I just run from one activity or commitment to the next one. I don't spend real quality time with anyone . . . especially you. This is hard to admit, but I confess that I often rush through my devotional time or sometimes skip it altogether. Too often my prayer time is spent in the car rushing to the next "very important" thing on my agenda.

Here's the thing—I know that Jesus is the example for my life, and even with people constantly clamoring for his attention, he made rest a priority. He made time with you a priority. He knew he would be better able to serve the people if he was rested and well connected to you. I suppose it's okay to use drive time to pray, but I want to better follow Jesus's example. So, help me prioritize my life so I have quality time to spend with you with no distractions. Time when I can meditate and listen and read your Word. Time to hear you speak to me.

I love you, Father. I want to spend time with you.

Jesus said, "Let's go off by ourselves to a quiet place and rest awhile." He said this because there were so many people coming and going that Jesus and his apostles didn't even have time to eat.

Mark 6:31

92

Blessings Overflowing

Father,

Luke 6:38 always reminds me of brown sugar. "Pressed down, shaken together and running over" (NIV). I remember my mom teaching me to make chocolate chip cookies and showing me how to measure the brown sugar by pressing more and more into the measuring cup. That's a sweet, sweet memory. The image is like your blessings of joy, hope, and peace—pressed down, shaken together, and always, always running over. They keep coming and coming.

I am grateful for your overflowing grace, peace, and blessings. Your love is deeper, wider, and fuller than I can comprehend. Oh Father, remind me of this every day so that I don't get weighed down by disappointments, struggles . . . life. That happens too easily. I pray that from the moment I open my eyes in the morning I will recognize all you do for me—the daily blessings I take for granted and the majestic ones that surprise me.

Then, Father, remind me to give to others with the same selfless generosity you show me. Give me the capacity to never hold back from blessing others. Father, I long to be a "brown sugar blessing" to others because you are constantly giving to me.

Give, and it will be given to you. A good measure, pressed down, shaken together and running over, will be poured into your lap. For with the measure you use, it will be measured to you.

Luke 6:38 NIV

93

Putting on God's Armor

My loving Father,

Satan is sneaky but brutal. He's subtle but attacking. He never stops trying to pull me away from you. He's constantly attacking me at every turn through work issues, relationships, and one crisis after another. Oh God, I'm weary. I feel beaten down, helpless, and too weak to fight anymore. I've tried fighting on my own, but I don't have the strength. I don't have the persistence, and I give up too easily.

But I don't need to fight on my own—your help is available to me. All along I have only needed to come to you because you've promised me help and protection. You've even provided armor for me to wear as protection in the battle against Satan. The amazing armor of God. I just need to put it on.

Father, I claim that armor right now. I claim that if I intentionally stay in your Word, learning and absorbing, I will be able to trust its truth above all other "truths" that are thrown at me. I will use it to protect my thoughts and attitudes. I will hide in your righteousness, secure and protected from Satan's lies. I will seek peace founded on my faith in you.

I'm thankful, Father, for every piece of armor that you've provided for my protection. It shows how very much you love me.

Put on the full armor of God, so that you can take your stand against the devil's schemes.

Ephesians 6:11 NIV

94

No Greater Love

Dear God,

I am so very thankful for your wonderful, sacrificial plan that makes possible the forgiveness of my sins. It's because of your loving plan that I can even know you. Because of your actions I am confident that I will someday be with you in heaven, enjoying your presence, worshiping you . . . for eternity. That's only possible because Jesus willingly endured the pain and humiliation of taking on my sin and the abuse heaped on him by religious leaders of his day. Oh Father, I deserved the punishment, not him. But he protected me because of his love.

I will never know a greater love than what you have shown me. Your amazing sacrifice makes the message of Scripture mean so much. It is truth. It is love. It is forgiveness. It is grace. Because of that, I give you my heart and my life. The only way I can repay you is with my sincere devotion and love.

Thank you for paying the price for my sin. Thank you for your constant, grace-filled forgiveness, showing me what real love looks like every single day. Thank you that your love changes me, grows me, makes me better and better. Thank you for all of it. I will never know a greater love than yours.

He was wounded and crushed
because of our sins;
by taking our punishment,
he made us completely well.

Isaiah 53:5 CEV

95

My Hiding Place

Dear God,

When life is just too much—and there are certainly times when it is—what a comfort it is to know that you're with me. You're always here. You are the good, unfailing constant in my life. Thank you for never turning away from me. Thank you for not giving up on me, even when I struggle with the same questions, doubts, and sins over and over. I try to learn and grow, but sometimes I take two steps forward and ten steps back. Still, when life is too much, it is an incredible comfort that you are with me. It's almost like climbing into your arms for a warm, loving, protective hug, knowing I am safely hidden from the stresses and crises of life.

Of course, those things will raise their heads again and again, but Father, you are my shield against the bad things that come. I know that you love me very much. Whatever I'm dealing with, you hold me close, allowing me to hide my tired, scared, hurting heart in your love. Oh Father, thank you for being my safe place, my hiding place. Thank you for loving me, comforting me, and protecting me even from myself. I love you, Lord.

God is a safe place to hide,
  ready to help when we need him.
We stand fearless at the cliff-edge of doom,
  courageous in seastorm and earthquake,
Before the rush and roar of oceans,
  the tremors that shift mountains.

Psalm 46:1–3 The Message

96

A Thankful Heart

Father,

Everything can change so quickly. Changes often leave me confused and frightened. Sometimes I think I've totally blown my relationship with you by my choices, words, or actions and that my usefulness to you is over. When relationships I value slip away or my career takes a strong left turn, I feel confused. Sometimes my interests and passions shift, and then I'm lost, almost drifting as I look for my footing again.

I long to be useful to you and to know my purpose in every stage of life, because yes, life changes are constant and often I have no control over those changes. I'm more grateful than ever that you have a plan for me. You already know what today, tomorrow, and a year from now will bring. In all those shifts and changes you are working out your good plan for my life. I'm so grateful that you are in control.

Thank you for giving me hope. Thank you for guiding my steps. Thank you for moving me and changing me (even when I resist) as you grow me into the woman you know I can be. I'm grateful that I don't have to blindly maneuver through life on my own but can trust you for purpose through every stage of my life.

"I know the plans I have for you," says the Lord. "They are plans for good and not for disaster, to give you a future and a hope."

Jeremiah 29:11

97

Sharing the Good News

My precious Lord,

I can see why the gospel is called Good News. Knowing you is a treasure, Father. You changed everything in my life. You saw me as I was but loved me enough to move me beyond that. You are making me a better woman every day. Through you I know a love and peace deeper than any human can give. I have strength and courage available to me that I know goes beyond myself. I have the hope of eternity with you in your glorious heaven. You give purpose to my days by giving me opportunities to use the passions and talents that make me who I am.

Father, this good news is too precious to be kept quiet. I must share it with others so that they, too, can have the opportunity to experience it. Give me courage to be brave enough to share. Give me your wisdom to know when to speak up. Give me the words to say that honestly convey who you are and how you love. I believe that Jesus is your Son, the Messiah, the answer to all I've searched for in my life. I know I am saved from a life of condemnation and eternity apart from you. Oh Lord, I want others to have that assurance too. Help me share.

If you openly declare that Jesus is Lord and believe in your heart that God raised him from the dead, you will be saved.

Romans 10:9

98

It Isn't All about Me

Dear Father,

It doesn't take much to set me off. Anger bubbles up in my gut until it explodes from my mouth. Ugliness, God. Hateful, hurtful words. Words that would crush me if hurled at me the way I hurl them at others. Too often I even feel justified in what I say, like I deserve to be angry because I've been wronged or hurt or cheated. I never expect my own anger to bounce back on me, but it does. It always does—through broken relationships, broken reputation, and guilt. There's always guilt. Even when I manage to swallow that bubbling anger and keep it from blasting forth, it eats at my insides. It comes out in sarcasm cleverly disguised as humor—which doesn't fool many.

Help me control my anger. Help me take a symbolic step back and try to see situations from others' viewpoints. Even if I don't agree, help me take "me" out of the situation—it isn't all about me anyway. Give me strength to let go . . . to walk away . . . to consider others' feelings before my own . . . to save friendships and relationships . . . with you, with others, and even with myself.

Don't be quick to fly off the handle.
Anger boomerangs. You can spot a fool
by the lumps on his head.

Ecclesiastes 7:9 The Message

99

Prayer against Satan

Father God,

I praise you for your power. Oh God, more than ever we need your power to help us fight against the Evil One. He has sneakily crept his way into so much of our world. He blinds the eyes of even those who know you. He confuses those who want to know you. Sometimes he is quiet and slow. Sometimes he is loud and powerful. Oh God, he must be stopped.

I pray, Father, that you will bind Satan's power. I pray that you will shut him down. I pray that your people will join hands and kneel together in prayer to stop him. I pray that you will free the hearts and minds of the ones he has blinded. I pray that you will protect your children by opening our eyes and hearts to Satan's tricks. I pray that we will be encouraged to put on the armor you have given us through your Word. I pray that we will see the urgency of stopping him and helping others know you.

Oh God, he has no power over you. He is not equal to you. Father, bind him. Strengthen your children to stand together to honor you, serve you, and share the message of your gospel with all,

---

For we are not fighting against flesh-and-blood enemies, but against evil rulers and authorities of the unseen world, against mighty powers in this dark world, and against evil spirits in the heavenly places.

Ephesians 6:12

100

A Life of Peace

Oh Father,

How I long for peace. I need peace that lasts longer than just a second. Peace that sinks deep into my soul, settling there. Peace that gives me honest satisfaction and contentment with my life, even when things aren't perfect. Peace because I know I'm loved and cared for by the God of the Universe and that I'm exactly where I'm meant to be. Peace that encourages me to celebrate the joys and successes of others without becoming jealous of them.

There it is—I've seen how jealousy and envy destroy. Oh God, I've seen it and even experienced the damage envy does to relationships. I've seen it break family relationships. I've seen it end friendships and damage work relationships. When envy takes over, peace is gone and little survives. Envy makes me sick—emotionally and physically.

Lord, I ask you to help me get a handle on envy. Show me how to push it out of my heart so that I make room for your peace to fill me. Your peace that makes room for satisfaction and contentment. Peace that allows me to know that I am who you made me to be and I'm doing just what you want for me.

A heart at peace gives life to the body,
but envy rots the bones.

Proverbs 14:30 NIV

Index of Prayers by Topic

Carolyn Larsen is the bestselling author of more than fifty books for children and adults. She has been a speaker for women's events and classes around the world, bringing scriptural messages filled with humor and tenderness. For more information, visit carolynlarsen.com and follow her on Facebook.